JOSH McDOW[...]
THOMAS WILLIAMS

THE
RELATIONAL
WORD

A Biblical Design to Reclaim and Transform the Next Generation

GREEN KEY BOOKS

Holiday, Florida

THE RELATIONAL WORD
©2006 by Josh McDowell and Thomas Williams
ISBN: 1932587837
Cover graphics: Kirk DouPonce

Editorial assistance provided by The Livingstone Corporation (www.LivingstoneCorp.com). Project staff includes Mary Larsen and Linda Taylor.
Published by Green Key Books
2514 Aloha Place
Holiday, FL 34691

Library of Congress Cataloging-in-Publication Data

McDowell, Josh.
  The relational word: a biblical design to reclaim and transform the next generation / Josh McDowell, Thomas Williams.
     p. cm.
  Includes bibliographical references.
  ISBN 1-932587-83-7
  1. Spirituality. 2. Christian life. 3. Young adults—Religious life. 4. Word of God (Theology) 5. Bible—Evidences, authority, etc. 1. Williams, Thomas, II. Title.
  BV4501.3.M333 2006
  248.4—dc22

                                    2006017938

Printed in the United States of America.

07 08 09   5 4 3 2

To the "Firehouse Theologians"

Chris Frizzell, Haney Poynor, James Greer, Jeff Berryman, John Knox, Rudy Rountree, and Terry Bibb

Acknowledgments

No book comes into existence without the help and cooperation of many people. We express our heartfelt gratitude to those who worked with us to make this book possible. First, we thank our good friend and co-worker Dave Bellis for his overall management of the project from concept to finish, including pairing the two of us to write the book, handling all the business arrangements, and guiding the process to completion. We thank publisher Peter Castor for performing all the many tasks involved in bringing the book to the public; editors Mary Larsen and Linda Taylor of the Livingstone Corporation, and Green Key editor Krissi Castor for their excellent work in combing the knots out of the manuscript; reader Gene Shelburne for his insightful comments and stylistic suggestions; and designer Kirk DouPonce for the first-rate cover.

While the bulk of this book is truly a collaborative effort, the last three chapters on evidences in the Bonus Section are based solely on the research of Josh McDowell. We thank writer Kevin Johnson for assembling the material in these three chapters for inclusion in this book. Our sincere gratitude goes out to all of you who helped us in these many ways. We could not have done it without you.

— Josh McDowell
— Thomas Williams

Contents

Part I. How God Reveals Himself to Us

    Chapter 1: Why Doesn't the Bible Make More Difference in Our Lives? 3

    Chapter 2: The Big Picture: The Hidden Truth about Christianity 19

    Chapter 3: Passing the Baton 33

Part II. Revealing God to the Next Generation

    Section 1: *God Understands Us Intimately* 45

        Chapter 4: Our Need for Intimate Understanding 47

        Chapter 5: How Christ Meets Our Need for Intimate Understanding ... 57

        Chapter 6: Modeling Intimate Understanding 69

    Section 2: *God Accepts Us Unconditionally* 87

        Chapter 7: Our Need for Unconditional Acceptance 89

        Chapter 8: How Christ Meets Our Need for Unconditional Acceptance 99

        Chapter 9: Modeling Unconditional Acceptance 111

    Section 3: *God Loves Us Sacrificially* 127

        Chapter 10: Our Need for Sacrificial Love 129

        Chapter 11: How Christ Meets Our Need for Sacrificial Love 139

        Chapter 12: Modeling Sacrificial Love 145

    Section 4: *God Relates to Us Continually* 157

        Chapter 13: Our Need for a Continuing Relationship 159

        Chapter 14: How Christ Meets Our Need for a Continuing Relationship 171

        Chapter 15: Modeling Continuing Relationships 183

Bonus Section. How We Know the Bible Is Reliable 193

    Chapter 1: Why We Must Have a Reliable Bible 197

    Chapter 2: The Bible Is Reliable: Internal Evidence 201

    Chapter 3: The Bible Is Reliable: Bibliographic Evidence 215

    Chapter 4: The Bible Is Reliable: External Evidence 229

Notes 243

About the Authors 249

PART I

How God Reveals Himself to Us

Why Doesn't the Bible Make More Difference in Our Lives?

It was well after seven o'clock in the evening when John Chadwick pulled into his garage. With a sigh, he grabbed the briefcase filled with papers he needed to finish that night and trudged toward the door to the kitchen. He could already hear the raised voices of his wife Ellen and his fourteen-year-old daughter Ashley. He entered the house just in time to see Ashley stomp up the stairs to her room, followed by the slam of her door.

"What was that all about?" asked John.

"Same old thing," Ellen sighed, shaking her head. "We finished dinner, and I just asked her to help clear the table. She said she had homework, but I insisted that she stay and help. She started complaining that I didn't care anything about her—that the only reason I even had her was to get a slave to do my work. I told her to talk more respectfully to me, reminding her that the Bible says to honor your father and mother, and things went downhill from there. Oh, John, I don't know what to do with that girl. I just want her to learn responsibility."

John shook his head and dropped wearily into his chair at the table as Ellen cleared the dishes from the family's just-finished meal. As he loaded his plate with casserole, now cold and lumpy, a loud, throbbing metallic sound suddenly rocked the house.

"Turn that thing down!" yelled John in a voice that lifted the rafters. But the noise continued. He slammed his fork to the table, stormed up the stairs to sixteen-year-old Hunter's room, burst through the door, and slapped the off button to his son's CD player. "I've told you a thousand times not to play this ridiculous music so loud. I don't know why you listen to this trash, but if you must, the least you can do is have the courtesy to use your headphones. Don't you know there are other people in this house besides you? We'd like to be able to hear each other talk. Yet you ignore what we've taught you from the Bible: 'Do unto others as you would have them do unto you.' But what the Bible says doesn't mean anything to you, does it?"

Hunter merely sat at his computer staring at the screen in sullen silence as his father glared at him and then walked out of the room.

"I don't know what we're going to do with that boy," sighed John as he sat again at the table.

"I know. I'm really worried about him," said Ellen. "He never comes out of his room. He just sits up there with that noise he calls music and surfs the Internet. And John, I suspect he may be breaking through the firewall and going to porn sites."

John did not reply. He was already tired and had a mountain of paperwork ahead of him. He couldn't deal with family problems again tonight.

John and Ellen were concerned about their kids for other reasons as well. Hunter's grades had been falling. He had brought home C's in math and English last semester. Over and over John had talked to his son about his grades, his music, and his time on the Internet; and his mother had pushed him about reading his Bible and getting involved in the church youth group. But the boy just sat through the lectures sullen and unresponsive.

Ashley, on the other hand, was anything but sullen. She openly rebuffed her parents' frequent urgings to read the Bible and their attempts to improve her behavior by quoting Scripture to her.

The Chadwicks had found that both children had lied to them more than once. Just last week, Ashley told them she was going to a PG movie and went instead to one with a heavy R-rating that John had forbidden. Hunter lied about a party he attended where drugs were used extensively. And one of the reasons for Hunter's falling math grades was that the teacher caught him cheating on an exam and gave him a zero on the test. When John confronted his son, he didn't think he had done anything all that bad. "Everyone does it all the time," he said. "I just happened to get caught."

John and Ellen have tried to instill into their children Christian values and right behavior from the pages of the Bible. They have told them how important it is to obey God's commandments: Certain things are right, others are wrong, and God is not pleased when we disobey him. They did not just sit idly by as they saw their children slipping away; they tried in many ways to change the direction of their kids—warning them that their behavior could be jeopardizing their souls, imposing mandatory church attendance, Bible readings, lectures, groundings, restrictions—but none of it has worked. They are frustrated, and they don't understand. Both are respected, hardworking, Bible-believing members of their church. John is even a deacon, and Ellen is on several committees and sings in the choir. Still, in spite of their commitment to church and the Bible and their repeated admonishments and discipline, John and Ellen can see that they are losing their children.

The Chadwick family is more typical than we want to believe. Similar behavior is prevalent in Christian households all across the country. Parents are frustrated because their children's churchgoing, their youth activities, and their teachings from the Bible don't seem to be making any difference. And they are right; for the most part, it isn't. Recent statistics from a nationwide study show no more than a four-percentage point difference between the moral and ethical behavior of Christian young people and their non-Christian peers.[1] George Barna's research shows that the lives of 98% of professed born-again young people do not reflect Christlike attitudes and behaviors.[2] Why is this happening? Why isn't our teaching about Christianity making any difference in the lives of today's young people? Why is the behavior of Christian young people essentially no different from their unchurched peers?

The Great Misunderstanding

The answer is that most of our kids, even those who seem to be active Christians, have distorted beliefs about God, Christianity, and the Bible. And those beliefs greatly affect their attitudes and behavior. They are adopting a religious outlook based on a huge misunderstanding of what Christianity is about, and consequently, they are not experiencing a transformed relationship with Christ so that "the old way of living has disappeared. A new way of living has come into existence" (2 Corinthians 5:17).

While many of our young people—and many adults for that matter—may believe the Bible provides some excellent guidance, it does not occur to them that its primary purpose is to introduce them to the person of Christ so they can come into a relationship with him. It does not occur to them that a relationship with Christ has any real meaning other than as a metaphoric religious phrase that probably means just to obey his rules and try to be good and that makes God happy with you. It does not occur to them that a relationship with Christ can be real or that it can provide the dynamic for their life and give it purpose and meaning. Rather, they believe that direction, purpose, and meaning must be created from within themselves.

An illumining example of this mindset at work was depicted in the popular nineties movie *City Slickers*. In this film, Billy Crystal plays Mitch Robbins, a man reaching middle age and plunging into a midlife crisis. He feels that his life is falling apart. His job has become boring and meaningless, he sees no purpose in anything he does, and it's all beginning to erode his relationship with his wife and family. To help him find himself, Mitch's wife enrolls him in a "dude" cattle drive led by a tough old trail boss named Curly, played by Jack Palance. Mitch is in awe of Curly's overpowering presence, command, and control. The old cowboy seems to have it all together. Curly, knowing that Mitch is floundering about in search of meaning, tells him, "You know what the secret of life is?" He holds up a single finger and says, "One thing . . . just one thing." Mitch asks what that "one thing" is, but Curly tells him, "That's what you've got to figure out." Curly dies shortly afterward, and Mitch remains puzzled about what the "one thing" could be. Finally, after completing the cattle drive against great odds, he is convinced that he has the answer. He tells his two friends, "I know what it is." When they ask for an explanation, he says, "That's what you have to figure out. It's something different for everybody. It's whatever is most important to you."

That is the postmodern answer to meaning and purpose. The "one thing" in your life is whatever you choose to make it. The current wisdom is that there is no single, overarching "one thing," so you must find one that works for you. Find a cause, something to dedicate yourself to, and make it your "one thing." That will give you meaning and purpose in life. Today's culture treats this idea as a profound insight, but it is really no solution at all. Many people invest themselves in several "one things." When one fails they find another and then another and then another. And ultimately all of them fail. Not one of the one things gives lasting meaning and purpose. With no real absolutes to guide them, this incessant groping about for something that has real meaning is the best the culture can offer.

The One Thing the Bible Reveals

Whatever is wrong in the Chadwick's household, we can't fault the parents for a failure to read and emphasize the importance of the Bible. John and Ellen are thoroughly convinced that it is the Word of God. They have read it, they have believed it, and they have tried to follow it. They even believe that it teaches them the true "one thing." So what could they be doing wrong? Why isn't their commitment to the Bible working for their family? It's because in spite of their commitment to the Bible, they have not yet found the true "one thing."

The Bible is making no difference in the Chadwicks' lives because they are missing its main point. They are making a critical mistake commonly made by most Christians today. What is the "one thing" the Bible offers? Survey almost any slice of Christians—youth or adult—and this answer will percolate to the top: "The Bible is a rule book." They think the "one thing" the Bible gives us is a set of rules to live by to improve our lives.

Indeed the Bible does present an abundance of excellent rules. It gives many beneficial instructions for living right and avoiding pitfalls. "Every Scripture passage is inspired by God. All of them are useful for teaching, pointing out error, correcting people and training them for a life that has God's approval" (2 Timothy 3:16). Yet for all of the guidance and instruction we can glean from the Bible, setting forth rules is not at the core of what it is all about.

For many other Christians, the "one thing" the Bible provides is a "road map to heaven." They see the primary purpose of religion and the goal of Christians as getting to heaven. Indeed, the Bible does show the way to heaven. As Peter said to Jesus, "Your words give eternal life" (John 6:68). The Bible conveys to us the words of Jesus that point us to heaven. But while the Bible is both a guide for living a good life and gives trustworthy direction to heaven, neither of those functions is the "one thing" that defines its true purpose.

I, Josh, discovered the true purpose of Scripture when I set out as a university student to refute Christianity.* I aimed to discredit the Bible by disproving its historical reliability. I reasoned that if the document containing the accounts of Christ could be exposed as historically inaccurate, the claims of Christ would be invalidated and the foundation of Christianity would crumble.

I failed in that quest, of course, because the evidences convinced me that the Bible is historically reliable—unquestionably so. Yet in my failure I experienced far more than I bargained for: I came face-to-face with the big truth—the "One Thing"—that the Bible reveals.

I found that the Bible gives us more than rules or a road map; it reveals a *person.* Through Scripture, God introduces himself to

---

* The personal experiences related in this book come from the lives of both Josh McDowell and Tom Williams. From this point on, however, anytime the personal pronoun is used without specific identification, it refers to Josh.

us. Through the Bible, we can come to know who God is, what he intends for us, what he expects from us, and how much he loves us. The Bible's first purpose and overarching theme is to unveil the person of God. That's it. That's the "One Thing" that the Bible reveals.

God revealed his desire for us to know him personally when he said to Hosea the prophet: "I want you to know me." Jesus himself affirmed this when he said, "This is eternal life: to know you, the only true God, and Jesus Christ, whom you sent" (John 17:1–3).

What did Jesus mean when he said that eternal life is found in *knowing* God? Obviously, knowing God isn't a mere intellectual understanding that he exists. Satan and his fallen angels know that he exists and that knowledge terrifies them. When Jesus says that eternal life is to know God, by *knowing* he means an intimate, relational connection—being one with God. "My prayer," Jesus said, "is that they will be one, just as you and I are one, Father—that just as you are in me and I am in you, so they will be in us, and the world will believe you sent me" (John 17:21, NLT). Knowing God intimately to the point of being one with him is life—eternal life, and it defines our purpose and meaning for existence.

In order to draw us into that relational connection, every person on earth was created with an irresistible longing to know and be known intimately. We all feel it—an intense craving to connect on a deep emotional level, a yearning to belong, a yearning for someone to discover the real person inside us, to want us, cherish us, and value us for the person we really are. Beneath their rebellious behavior, this is even what the Chadwick children really want. It is what every young person, child, and adult in this world really wants. We have a built-in aversion to aloneness. Connectedness with the right person brings meaning and completeness to the human heart.

The drive to satisfy this need for relationship is the underlying compulsion behind most of what we do, though often we don't recognize the true need beneath the compulsion. Homes like the

Chadwicks' are in turmoil because the kids—and possibly even the parents to one degree or another—have bought into the same lie as Mitch Robbins, the lie that they can find the answer to this fundamental human need on their own terms. Instead of recognizing their need for relationship with Christ and with each other, the Chadwicks try to find meaning in their own ways. John immerses himself in his work and business relationships. Ellen tries to find meaning in being good by the rules of the Bible and relationships in committees and church functions. Hunter loses himself in a world of illusory relationships on his computer and in his music. Ashley shuts out her family and seeks relationships with her peers.

But humans cannot find the answer to this relational need to connect to another on their own terms because the need was placed in our hearts by God himself, and He did so for one primary purpose: *to draw us into an intimate relationship with him that enables us to reflect his character and nature.* He created us to bear his likeness (Genesis 1:26–27), and only in continual relationship with him can we reflect that likeness and fulfill our purpose. That is why it is our intimate relationship with God that defines the essence of who we are.

Scripture is the means by which God has chosen to introduce and reveal himself to us initially so we can come to experience that intimate relationship with him. From cover to cover, the Bible shows us that he is a relational God who "would speak to Moses personally, as a man speaks to his friend" (Exodus 33:11). He is "a God who is passionate about his relationship with you" (Exodus 34:14, NLT). And Scripture tells us that his name is "love" (1 John 4:7).

From Genesis to Revelation, the Bible reveals the loving heart of a God who wants to be in relationship with us so that we can enjoy all that his love offers. Yes, the Bible contains rules, and yes, it provides a road map. But the rules and the directions are not the "one thing" the Bible is all about. The sole purpose of the rules and the map is to lead us into relationship with God. And that relationship with him is the "one thing."

The True Meaning of the Bible

In the modern age with its emphasis on reason, categories, and systems, there is a tendency to focus on the hard data of the Bible—its rules and directions—and to systematize all of it into a religious dogma. This tendency has led many to focus as much or even more on the Bible itself than on the God whom the Bible reveals. This is a huge mistake, of course, because as valuable as the Bible is to us, its value is not inherent within itself. Contrary to what we often hear in many of our churches, the Bible contains no power of its own. It is not our only source of faith. It is not the sole revelation of God to man. All these ideas comprise the great misunderstanding of the Bible, and they lead us to misuse it.

You will see as you read on that we are not discounting the immense importance of the Bible at all. We are merely saying that it is not an end in itself but rather a means to an end. The nineteenth-century Scottish author and preacher George MacDonald, whose writings significantly influenced C. S. Lewis, stated it well when he wrote, "But herein is the Bible itself greatly wronged. It nowhere lays claim to be regarded as *the* Word, *the* Way, *the* truth. The Bible leads us to Jesus, the inexhaustible, the ever unfolding Revelation of God. It is Christ 'in whom are hid all the treasures of wisdom and knowledge,' not the Bible, save as leading to Him."[3]

When we miss this core truth—that the Holy Scripture reveals a Holy God who desires an intimate relationship with us—we miss the Bible's main point and primary purpose. Jesus understood that it is possible to study Scripture diligently and yet miss its relational message. He warned the Pharisees, "You search the Scriptures because you believe they give you eternal life. But the Scriptures point to me! Yet you refuse to come to me so that I can give you this eternal life" (John 5:39–40, NLT).

I'm afraid that all too many pastors, teachers, and youth workers would say they study the Bible to present the truth of God to others rather than absorb its truth themselves to become more intimate with Christ. I know how easy it is to slip into this error. When I encounter young people who face crushing pain resulting from their wrong choices, my heart wells up with eagerness to share the Bible as a handbook for living. I want to help them learn the benefits of believing right and making right choices. Yet I constantly remind myself that doing right comes not from rules but from being in right relationship with God. When we present the Bible to young people not just as a rule book or road map but as his call to enter into an intimate relationship with him, we unveil God's full plan for them.

A transformed life conformed to the "image of his Son" does not come from using the Scripture as a suggestion manual or self-help book to create a privately held truth customized to fit us personally. It does not come from trying to obey the Bible as a set of rules or by following its principles and trying to live a good life. Living a Christlike life occurs when we enter into intimacy with Christ, submit ourselves to the Holy Spirit, and make him at home in our hearts. The only way to live a Christlike life is to let him live it through us by the power of his Holy Spirit living in us.

Don't let anything we've said above about the ways we misuse the Bible lead you to think it is unimportant. It is extremely, even crucially important. For most of us, it is our first introduction to the identity of God. Of course, he does reveal himself to us in other ways. We've all learned much about the character of God from nature and much about the love of God reflected in the lives of others. He also reveals himself to us by writing his law upon our hearts (Romans 2:15; Hebrews 10:16). But through the Bible, God specifically and unambiguously identifies himself as the power behind it all. Through the Bible, God says to us in essence, "I have preserved for you my written revelation as a lens to see me for who I am. Read its pages to know me. Become intimate with me, and, through our close relationship together, you will enjoy true meaning in living."

As long as we present the Bible to our youth as a religious system or only as a set of wise and useful teachings, they will evaluate it not as a universally true revelation of the one true God but as one alternative in a sea of competing truths. If they take it seriously at all, they will do what the pervasive philosophy of the postmodern culture teaches them to do. They will lock in on any part of the Bible that seems to work for them and reject the rest. And they will resist the claim that Christianity is the one true religion because the culture has conditioned them to reject any claim to exclusive truth as intolerant—an exercise of power on the part of one group to gain control over others.

We must present Scripture not as another religious system but as an introduction to the one, true God, communicating his intense love and desire for relationship. It is crucial that our young people understand the primary difference between Christianity and all other religions. Once they understand that difference, it should produce a life change. Buddhism, Hinduism, Islam, Confucianism, and all other religions are based on the teachings of their founders. Remove their founders from the picture, and the religion still stands intact because the teachings themselves are the essence of the religions. But remove Christ from Christianity and the religion falls. Christianity is like no other religion. Its essence is not its teachings but the person of Christ himself. Christianity is not a call to learn a new system of how to be a better person or live a better life; it was not conjured up as a workable explanation for life's unfathomable mysteries. It was not developed by human philosophers as a system of ethical thought to define behavior. It was not worked out and fitted to humanity's needs as a therapy for coping. It is a call to be one with him and in that oneness to achieve the "one thing" that everyone on earth really wants and needs—complete fulfillment of all desires in an eternal relationship of pure love. Once we make that intimate connection and enter a relationship with God, the teachings of the Bible become invaluable guides to aligning our lives with his will and character.

Now, if what the Bible reveals is not true, then the culture is right; Christianity has no business claiming to be the one truth.

But if the claims of the Bible are objectively true, then God is exactly who he claims to be: the one and only God in existence who tells us that only in relationship to him will we find fulfillment, meaning, and love. If this claim is true, then it doesn't matter whether it is politically correct. It doesn't matter that it outrages cultural conventions by claiming to be exclusive. It doesn't matter that it appears intolerant of other beliefs. If it's true, *it's true*, and nothing else matters.

Christianity is indeed *true* in the rock-bottom sense of the word. It comes to us in the hard, unchangeable, immutable package of solid fact that can be verified historically. God actually did come to earth as a man with skin, bone, fingernails, and hair. A real and personal God who is literally alive now wants to come into the life of every human who opens his or her heart to him. This is not a metaphor or a myth or a vivid analogy designed to convey a philosophic abstraction; it is a literal truth that we mean in exactly the words we use to express it: God died on a cross to remove from you the guilt of sin, and he is available to live in our lives, giving us an intimate, loving relationship with him from this moment forward. Our young people must know these facts. They must know that the truth of the Bible is real and objective, and our opinions about it are immaterial.

Therefore when God speaks, we'd better listen. When he says he wants to transform us into his image, we do well to submit to the operation. If the one God who created the universe designed us, it makes sense that only he and no one else can tell us how to fulfill our purpose and bring us to a life of incredible, unending joy. When this monolithic fact dawns on our young people, the postmodern picture will flicker and fade from the screen.

Since it is so crucial to the challenges of the postmodern culture that our kids understand that the Bible is objectively true, we are adding a bonus section at the end of this book giving evidences of the Bible's validity. We believe this will provide a valuable reference tool for adults leading this generation to the truth.

The One Thing We All Need

If Christ offers the "one thing" that humans desperately desire and need, then why doesn't this generation see Christianity as relevant? Why don't people flock to churches? One reason is that many don't perceive a relationship with Christ as the "one thing" that "satisfies every need there is" (Acts 17:25, NLT). They don't think a man who lived two thousand years ago, the Bible, or the church has any relevance to the real world or any means of satisfying their real needs. It may be that what they have seen in the lives of many Christians has turned them off and made them unreceptive. "If she's a model of what Christianity is like, who needs it!" If the lives of Christians don't reflect joy, peace, and love, why should people believe Christianity could possibly offer anything leading to true happiness or deep meaning?

Another obstacle to belief may be the enormity of Christianity's claims. Those claims seem incredible to people brought up in the modern age. "Do you mean to tell me that insignificant creatures such as you and I can know personally the supernatural being that created the universe and life on this planet?" We admit it: the claim that we can know God intimately is astounding. It gives one chill bumps to think about it. Of course, we don't claim that we finite humans can know everything about God any more than your small children can know everything about you. We may not be able to know God fully, but we can know his heart truly. He has revealed it to us in three spectacular ways. First, he came down from heaven to live and die as one of us. Two thousand years ago, "the Word became human and lived among us" (John 1:14). Second, he revealed his heart in words written in human language. Seventeen hundred years ago God gave us the New Testament as a written revelation of his character. Third, he has revealed his heart through the most intimate revelation of himself in giving his Holy Spirit to live in us and provide loving directive for our lives.

There is one more way that God reveals his heart, and that will be the primary subject of the rest of this book. He reveals himself through the lives of committed Christians. Our charge is to model Christ for others to see so that they can come to know him through us.

As families and individuals take seriously their challenge to represent Christ to others, our young people can see as never before the relational heart of God. They will see it in action. They will see it up close and personal. They will see it housed in humanity that they know and love. And that has real impact. When parents, teachers, and youth workers model God's heart for relationship to our kids and those around them, we have a realistic hope of reclaiming an entire generation for the kingdom of God in spite of the pervasive influence of the culture. It's not just a dream. We can truly have young people who live as "children of God without fault in a crooked and depraved generation, in which [they] shine like stars in the universe" (Philippians 2:15, NIV).

Think of the possibilities. What if, instead of using the Bible as a rule book to browbeat their kids into obedience, the Chadwick parents used it to introduce Hunter and Ashley to the heart of a loving Christ, guiding them into a relationship with God's Holy Spirit and modeling to their children the kind of love that God has for them? Let's look at how Mr. Chadwick's arrival at home could look if he and his wife were to follow this course of action:

> It was a little before six o'clock in the evening when John Chadwick pulled into his garage. Even before he opened the door to the kitchen, he could hear the laughter of his wife Ellen and their fourteen-year-old daughter Ashley. He entered the house to see Ashley sweeping up a pile of broken glass and pot roast as she and her mother giggled.
>
> "What's so funny?" asked John.
>
> "Oh, you should have seen us a moment ago," said Ellen. "Hunter waxed the kitchen floor this afternoon, and it was so slick that when Ashley got the roast out

of the oven the heel of her shoe slipped, and she did a little impromptu imitation of Michael Flatley. You've never seen such a dance! When I tried to catch her, we got tangled, and both of us landed on the floor." The mother and daughter went into another fit of giggles.

John smiled. "I'm glad you find something funny in the fact that we have no dinner tonight."

"Hey," said Ellen, "when you have a daughter who comes down and helps you fix the meal every night and a son who waxes your floor and whistles while doing it, what's a missed meal now and then?" She hugged her daughter as she spoke.

"You are quite right," said John, wrapping both of them in his arms. "Call Hunter down. Let's celebrate that blessing and let Chili's cook our dinner tonight. And afterward, we might even take in a movie."

Does this scene sound like a fantasy too good to be true? It isn't. It could be the picture of every family in America if parents would simply model the relationship they have with Christ to their children. How do you do that? It's not as hard as you think.

In this book, we want to demonstrate how parents, grandparents, youth leaders, coaches, teachers, and others involved in the lives of young people can make Christ real to the next generation. We want to give you practical help in introducing God to them so that they will come to understand his loving heart and desire an intimate relationship with him. In the chapters that follow, we will...

• Set the foundation for your relationship by showing from the pages of Scripture the big picture of what God is all about with us. You may be surprised at how little it has to do with propositional theology and how much it has to do with sheer love.

• Identify from the pages of Scripture four of the most basic relational needs common to every person on earth and show how a relationship with Christ meets every one of them fully.

- Discover how simply becoming a walking model of Christ is the most powerful and effective way to meet the relational needs in the lives of our families and neighbors.

- As a bonus, we have added a significant section to the back of this book giving you basic but highly effective ways of showing your young people powerful evidences supporting the reliability of the Bible so that they will have confidence that what the Bible reveals about Christ is accurate.

CHAPTER 2

The Big Picture: The Hidden Truth about Christianity

Since a huge misunderstanding about the nature of Christianity misleads many of our young people to dismiss it or treat it as a periphery to their lives, it's imperative that we have the correct understanding firmly set in our minds. We have said that the essence of Christianity is not in its doctrines or its theological system, as important as those may be; it is actually all about a relationship with God. What does that mean? Doctrines and systems have value when they clarify God's purpose to us, but they can easily become our primary focus and obscure the true intent of the Bible. In this chapter, we want to rise above the haze of all the doctrines and dogma that have accumulated around Christianity to give you a clear look at the big picture of God's relational intention from the beginning.

The core truth of Christianity is really more of a story than a system. Strip away all of the elements that cause people to think of it as a system—the doctrines, theologies, laws, and other complexities that distract us from its central message—and you have a compelling drama. Young people today tend to think in stories rather than systems, so the drama of God's relationship with mankind should have an impact on their hearts and minds. In the telling of this story, we will uncover the central truth that will set the stage for everything we have to say in the rest of this book.

The Creation Story

The colorful cycle of poems *God's Trombones* by James Weldon Johnson begins, "And God stepped out on space. And he looked around and said, 'I'm lonely. I'll make me a world.'"[1] Allowing for a little poetic license, Mr. Johnson was onto something with his opening line. Of course, God could never be literally lonely. The essence of his being is an intimate unity of three personalities bonded by love. He is complete within himself and never had any void in his existence that needed filling. Yet his infinite capacity to love led him to desire more living beings for his love to enfold.

We humans can understand this desire because we share it. Like God, we delight in having other living creatures around us to lavish our affection upon. Though young married couples are deeply in love and blissfully wrapped up in each other, almost universally they want children. They want to expand their love to include others like themselves, whom they beget and bear "in their own image."

Every couple knows that bringing children into the world is a risky venture. The cost will be great in many ways. Children take time, money, dedication, and sacrifice. And the cost can be even greater. It can mean nursing them through serious illness, financial stress, the heartbreak of alienation, and even the overwhelming tragedy of loss through death. Yet couples almost always want children. Why? Because we are created in the image of God, and it is his nature to want his love to expand and enfold others.

God knew the cost of love could be great. It could mean the tragedy of alienation and even death. Yet this all-powerful, self-sufficient God desired to have other creatures to love who were capable of responding to him and loving him back.

Acting on this desire, God decided to create a race of creatures called humans. Like parents-to-be setting up a nursery, he first created the earth as an environment for his humans. You've seen the nurseries of newborns—lavishly furnished with every conceivable need to keep the baby happy and comfortable—furniture, toys, pictures, and blankets, all wildly colorful and spotlessly clean. The new earth was like that—a sparkling jewel of lavish beauty and pristine perfection. Nature was in perfect balance, benign and friendly. Animals roamed about in idyllic harmony. The climate was springlike and ideal year-round. The horrors of nature that ravage the world today were unheard of. Death, pain, hunger, disease, hurricanes, tornadoes, floods, drought, famine, heat waves, or artic freezes did not exist.

In the midst of this perfect environment, God prepared a beautiful garden in a lush setting between two rivers, and he filled it with flourishing greenery and every kind of fruit-bearing tree. Then as his crowning act of creation, God formed the human man and woman and placed them within this ideal setting.

Adam, the first man, was the model of ideal manhood—strong, healthy, noble, and godlike. His wife Eve was gorgeous, the loveliest creature ever to walk the face of the earth. They were exactly what each of us dreams of being—beautiful, strong, healthy, and perfect in every way. They experienced no pain, disease, sorrow, illness, accidents, or even death. The man and woman were deeply in love and in complete harmony with each other. Adam and Eve, living in Eden, loving each other and caring for the earth, were ecstatically happy. Had we seen them in Eden, we might have found it hard to resist the temptation to fall down and worship them as gods, for they perfectly reflected the very image of God.

Imagine spending a day with Adam and Eve. At sunrise they awoke refreshed and cheerful, without a trace of morning grumpiness. They hugged and kissed each other and then marched off to work in the garden. Though they applied themselves diligently to every task, they never tired. In fact, they seemed to find immense joy in tending and shaping their property and nourishing and guiding the creatures that fawned on them. When they grew hungry, they paused and ate from the abundant food growing all about them and quenched their thirst from crystal streams. As evening approached, Adam and Eve left their work, plunged into a clear lake and swam about for half an hour and then dried off by chasing through a cool woods unblighted with stickers or poison ivy. Reaching the blossom-covered bower that was their home, they sat drinking fresh juice from a coconut shell as they eagerly awaited the highlight of their day.

"Is he coming yet?" Eve asked, looking down the path toward the woods.

"I don't hear him," Adam replied. "It may be a little early."

They sipped and talked of plans for a grove of trees near the waterfall to the east. After a few minutes, Eve looked again toward the woods, her eyes bright with anticipation.

"I still don't see him," she said.

"Listen," replied Adam. "I think I hear something."

They both kept still and listened, and in moments the familiar, soft sound of movement through the grass was unmistakable.

"Oh, he's coming!" Eve could not contain her excitement. She bounded joyfully up the path as Adam closed the distance behind her. They ran to God like children to a father returning home at the end of a workday. And until sundown, the happy pair walked the paths of the garden and chatted with their creator as their souls within them burned with ecstatic joy.

Far-fetched? Fanciful? Unrealistic? Not at all. While the details of this scene are fictional, it is a true picture of how Adam and Eve responded to God. They looked forward to his presence with all the anticipation of a lover. And the amazing thing is that God also delighted in them. Just as a mother delights in the smile of her infant when it looks into her face, God delights in the love of his human creatures (Psalm 18:19). He loved Adam and Eve with an incredible passion and derived great pleasure from their relationship with him (see Proverbs 11:20). This intimate, joyful relationship between God and mankind, with love flowing in both directions, was his intention not merely for this first couple, but for all humanity for all time.

Intimacy with God was not only the source of all joy and harmony for Adam and Eve; it was also the source of meaning for their lives. God gave to them the exalted honor of carrying his own life at the center of their beings. He breathed his own Spirit into the man (Genesis 2:7), giving humankind an intimate connection with him that no other creature had. Man and woman were God's representatives to all creation, bearing in their own beings the Spirit of God himself and showing his nature in everything they did. Their central purpose was to be God-carriers, which meant having the greatest love of their life within them at every moment. This intimate connection with God was the source of meaning for their lives and also the source of their joy.

We said above that when God created humans to love he took a risk. The risk was that they could choose to reject him. To be authentic, love must be free and voluntary. It cannot be forced. God loved Adam and Eve, and he wanted them to love him freely in return. Therefore, he did not plant in them an automatic, irresistible response mechanism that would force them to love him as instinct dictates the behavior of animals. Instead, he drew them to love him by giving them built-in desires for relationship that could be satisfied only in him. Thus drawn to God, they remained in relationship with him by their own free choice and loved him willingly. Only this kind of freedom could make the flow of love between God and mankind authentic.

This flow of love was God's ultimate intention for all humanity from creation forward. He created Adam and Eve and all their descendants to be ecstatically happy in a loving relationship with him forever. And in Eden, it all worked perfectly.

The Fall

Obviously, somewhere along the way something went wrong. This world we live in is hardly the garden of Eden. Far from delighting in God, many people today feel quite the opposite toward him. Some see God as something like a strict judge watching their every move with a stern, disapproving eye. Many find the idea of God so far-fetched that they don't even believe he exists. And even if he does exist, some think he is remote and uncaring—somewhere off in his distant heaven leaving them to struggle alone with problems that don't seem to have handles in a world filled with every kind of evil. What happened? How did we move from intimacy with God in the garden of Eden to alienation from him in today's messed-up world?

It started back in the distant recesses of time, even before the creation of Adam and Eve, when, as many theologians believe, one of God's finest creatures went bad. This creature, Satan by name, was the most beautiful of angels. But he grew proud of his magnificence and power and led a rebellion of fellow angels to challenge God for his throne. Angels loyal to God defeated Satan in a great war and threw him out of heaven. Seething with unquenchable anger, he sought vengeance by taking aim at God's grand project—the man and woman he created.

Taking the form of a serpent, which was in the beginning a beautiful creature, Satan slipped into Eden and sidled up to the stunningly beautiful woman, his iridescent scales glistening in the sun and his liquid eyes reflecting the wisdom of the ages.

"You think you're free," he said to her, "but do you call this freedom? Look at you; everything you do is in obedience to *him*." The creature rolled his eyes upward. "That God of yours has fooled you into thinking he made you in his likeness. But how can you think you're like him when he lords it over you the way he does? How can you call yourself free as long as he commands and you obey?"

"Oh, it's not like that at all," answered Eve. "He gives us the run of this garden, we have plenty of delicious food to eat, and he doesn't tell us to do anything except what makes us happy." She paused to wrap an ivy tendril around an oak limb. "Why should we want anything different?"

"But he did forbid you to eat one fruit, did he not?" replied the serpent. "Why can't you eat that sweet-smelling, bright, juicy morsel hanging on that tree right there?" he pointed to the thick, leafy tree in the center of the garden, its branches heavy with glistening orbs of fruit.

"Well, you're right. God did tell us not to eat that fruit," said the woman. "He said if we ate it we would die."

"Ah, but I happen to know better," replied Satan. "That fruit won't kill you. Do you want to know the real reason God forbids it?" He leaned close to her ear and lowered his voice to little more than a whisper, "It will give you knowledge that will make you equal to him, and he doesn't want rivals. He wants to keep you ignorant so he can control you. If you really want to be like God, assert yourself and eat that fruit. Let him know that you won't be kept down any longer. Get out from under his thumb—get out on your own and take control of your own destiny. Be your own person. Do your own thing."

The more Eve listened to that smooth-talking serpent, the more God's warning faded and his words became hazy. They didn't seem to make sense any more. Maybe that snake was right; God was holding back on her. Maybe she needed to break free of God to become her own person. With her heart racing, she reached out and gingerly touched the fruit. Nothing happened. She touched it again, tentatively closing her fingers around it. Nothing happened. Then she gripped it firmly, pulled it from the tree, and took a quick bite before she could change her mind. Immediately, she ran to Adam and managed to cajole him into eating it with her.

This disobedience to God's one prohibitive command was the first couple's declaration of independence. They chose to decide for themselves what was good instead of listening to God. They rejected the supremacy of God in favor of the supremacy of self, choosing to end their loving relationship with him and set themselves up as their own authority. And in the name of freedom, God sadly honored their choice. He withdrew his Spirit from their lives and allowed them the independence they had chosen.

But soon Adam and Eve learned that Satan had withheld a few important facts. Since they were created specifically to bear the Spirit of God and live in relationship with him, rejecting God emptied their lives of meaning. It also threw everything out of control. They thought that getting away from God would give them freedom, but they found that without him they were incapable of directing their own lives. Since everything about their design was geared, wired, and programmed to accommodate the presence of God in their lives, when they rejected him, the human operating system went out of sync. In disobeying, they had chosen what seemed good to them at the moment, overlooking the long-term effect of their choice. And that became the predominant pattern of decision-making for all humanity from that day forward. The result was chaos. Harmony ended in Adam and Eve's lives, not only with God but also with each other and with nature, to be replaced by pain, bitterness, isolation, and misunderstanding. Nature went out of control and became infested with weeds, rot, famine, death, and disaster. The human couple's intimacy with God became a tearful memory.

This tragic decision of Adam and Eve to rebel against God and run their own lives is known as the fall, and they passed on to all their descendents their fallen condition and alienation from God. As the apostle Paul explained, "When Adam sinned, sin entered the entire human race. Adam's sin brought death, so death spread to everyone, for everyone sinned" (Romans 3:25, NLT). In just a few generations after Adam, men and women lost all awareness of God. Since the one thing that could provide meaning in their lives was now missing, they felt an insatiable craving to fill the void, but they had no idea of what to look for or where to look. They tried to fill it by making their own gods, and they tried to find meaning in building great cities and nations. The history of humanity since the fall has been that of a search for what was lost in Eden—for that "one thing" that will give meaning and completeness to the human heart.

Enemies of God

The fall not only isolated men and women from God, it actually made them his enemies (Romans 5:10). Your first reaction to this may be that it seems a little extreme. We can understand why God would be saddened and disappointed by our rejection, but why would he suddenly see us as foes?

First of all, remember that Satan is a bitter enemy of God. So when we sinned, we inadvertently joined his rebellion and became traitors because we chose to side with God's enemy. That made us his enemies as well. But there is a larger answer, which we find in the concept of God's holiness.

Holiness gets little attention these days. We tend to be more interested in God's love and grace because of the benefit we get from them. But his holiness is an essential dimension of his character and a key to the position he had to take toward humanity after the fall. God's holiness means that he is absolute in his purity, perfection, and goodness. No flaw or hint of evil exists in him. Such perfect purity is the natural enemy to its opposite: evil and sin (Romans 5:9–10).

The concept of holiness seems extreme to us because we have little inkling of what absolute perfection means. In this fallen world, nothing is perfect, so we accept sin and imperfection as inevitable and think little of it. Most sins short of murder don't seem so bad "as long as they don't hurt anyone." But God must take a harder attitude toward all sin. If we could have experienced the world before the fall, we would understand that any sin at all—even a little white lie—is an outrage against the perfect order of the universe. God is absolutely perfect, and all creation must reflect his nature. He cannot allow sin to survive in his universe any more than you would allow disease-carrying rats to survive in your home. Otherwise, like a bacterial infection, sin would spread until all creation was ruined with the disease. To be true to his nature, God must clean up the earth and eradicate sin from it. Humans contaminated with sin became blights on his perfect creation and were, therefore, his enemies. They had to be marked for extermination.

God Couldn't Stand to Lose Us

But there was a hitch to this solution. Although the fall had made all humanity natural enemies to God, he was in love with us. As astounding as it seems, he could not stand the thought of losing us (John 3:16). The thought that you would not exist in his presence throughout eternity broke his heart. Therefore, he refused to accept Adam and Eve's rejection as the final word. He wanted us back, so he came after us.

But looming in his path stood that enormous obstacle: our sin. His heart ached to enfold us again, but he could not take us back without compromising his holiness—his innate perfect nature. The big dilemma was that sin had become part of *our* innate nature. It could not merely be extracted like an abscessed tooth. The infection of sin, passed on to us from Adam and Eve, contaminated our entire being just as some inoperable cancers spread throughout the body. No simple operation would cure it. Fallen humans could not merely straighten up and do right because their sinful behavior sprang from their innate nature, which had been permanently corrupted by sin. Men and women after Adam could not produce perfect behavior any more than pure water can be drawn from a sewer. The source had been contaminated. Only the death of every infected human would rid God's universe of sin. That is why Paul tells us that, "the reward for sin is death" (Romans 6:23).

The Bible presents the problem of our sin in another figure. Sin placed us under legal condemnation. In turning away from God, we had violated the law that gave our lives purpose, and God in his perfect justice had to pronounce the death penalty. The apostle Paul affirms the inevitability of God's judgment. "All of us must appear in front of Christ's judgment seat. Then all people will receive what they deserve for the good or evil they have done while living in their bodies" (2 Corinthians 5:10). The only way for us to escape death for our sins was for a perfect human to offer himself as a sacrifice for the rest of the race. Therefore, God's first need was a human being without a sin nature who was willing to sacrifice himself.

But there was the problem. In the course of nature, humanity could not produce a perfect human any more than a tiger could produce a grazing herbivore. Every human born since Adam automatically inherited his sin nature. If we were to be saved, however, a perfect, sinless human would have to be produced.

The Solution: God Became a Man

God's solution was to have himself born into the race of humanity. He would be naturally born of a human female but without the impregnating seed of a human male. By such a birth, a man could be produced who was both human and perfect. He would inherit his humanity from his mother, and he would be perfect, without the inheritance of Adam's sin nature, because he was of the seed of God. God born as a human could live as a perfect man—the prototype of what we could become—and he could die in our place as a man, thus meeting the requirements of justice and paying the price for sin.

God weighed all he had in the perfect beauty and harmony of heaven against his love for the humans he had created and said, in effect, "They are worth more to me than all this. I will leave the riches of heaven and the perfect love I know within the Trinity, and I will go down and rescue my beloved humans" (2 Corinthians 8:9). Amazingly, God chose us over heaven. At a specific time in history and a specific place on the map, God in the person of Jesus Christ stepped down from heaven and became one of us. The creator of the universe was born into our race as a baby and raised as the son of a tradesman. He took our sins as his own and allowed himself to be executed in our place. His death freed us from the guilt of sin, and with that contamination removed, God could restore to us the relationship lost at the fall.

You may look around you and say, "If Christ died to restore things as they were before the fall, it doesn't seem to have worked. This planet is a far cry from the garden of Eden. Pain and death still run rampant. Evil operates freely all around us.

God still seems remote and hard to find. Relationships are still hard to maintain and often turn sour. Why?"

The answer is that the death of Christ freed those who believe from the guilt of sin but not from the effects of it. God can now look on us as "legally" perfect because our guilt has been removed, but we are not yet functionally perfect. And we must still contend with the results of sin that has infected human lives since the fall, and that includes diseases, pain, and eventual physical death.

The reason is simple. Adam's free choice brought death on all of us, and for God to remove it would undo Adam's freedom. We humans would not be truly free if God stood by with a magic wand and poofed away the result of every sin we commit. If we were to retain our freedom, he had to let Adam's choice stand. Adam chose sin, and sin brought about death; therefore, death reigns over the human race. That means we must all live our lives on earth contending with the damaging effects of sin, and we must suffer the pain, disease, and physical death that Adam's sin imposed. The difference is that now this cloud of death has a silver lining. When we enter a relationship with Christ, he draws us into his perfection, and when we die, the effects of sin die with our bodies. God will then resurrect us with a new body free of sin and imperfection.

Restoring the Relationship

After Christ died, his followers buried him in a tomb near Jerusalem. Three days later, God resurrected him back to life. The disciples, who had been devastated by his death, were elated to have him back. But he could not stay. He had removed the barrier between God and humankind, and he now had to return to heaven so that his permanent replacement could come. This replacement was God himself in the form of the third member of the godhead, the Holy Spirit. In the person of the Holy Spirit, God would again enter the lives of all who chose to return to him, thus reversing the rebellion of Adam and restoring the intimate relationship with God that he intended at creation.

The Holy Spirit came first to the disciples of Jesus, and now he comes into the lives of everyone who invites him. When we return to God, he opens his arms in welcoming love, and all heaven rejoices. We don't have to wait for our resurrection into sinless perfection to restore our relationship with God. With Christ having removed the guilt of sin, God can declare us legally perfect the moment we choose to come back to him. And how does he get around the fact that he is holy and we have been contaminated by sin? He lets us "borrow" the perfection of Christ as our own until our own resurrection is accomplished (Philippians 3:9–12).

The word *religion* means to reconnect. You can see a hint of the word's meaning in its construction—to "re-ligature" or "re-ligament." But of all world religions, only one offers a way to reconnect with the personal God of the universe. The whole meaning of all we read in the Bible can be summed up as God's quest to restore the relationship between himself and mankind—to reconnect with us, to *re-ligature* the intimate oneness he intended. The Bible does not offer us a system or a set of do-it-yourself rules that will enable us to achieve goodness and go to heaven. It's not about rules; it's not about a map. It is about a person. The Bible tells the story of how that person went to incredible lengths to reestablish a relationship with people whom he loved too dearly to abandon to their own folly.

The Bible is the key not just to the one true religion but also to understanding the true nature of all reality. The truth about religion *is* the truth about reality. They can't be separated. Religion—reconnection with God—is life itself. Any concept of reality that does not place this truth at the core is utterly false. The overarching reality is that the God who created us is working in every life on earth in the hope that each person will reconnect in a loving relationship with him.

This is the big picture of what God is working to accomplish with humankind. We believe this picture can help you open young eyes to great truths that may not be clear to them. In the chapters that follow, we will draw from the principles we have explained here and show how you can reflect this truth to the next generation.

CHAPTER 3

Passing the Baton

I n the Olympic 400 meter relay race, four runners team up to carry a small baton the distance of 400 meters. Each runner carries the baton 100 meters, one lap around the oval track. As the runner completes a lap, he or she hands off the baton to the next runner. The passing of the baton is extremely important to completing the race. If any runner drops the baton, or if there is a failure in the process of one runner handing it off to the next, the race is over for that team. The baton must be carried to the finish line, or the race is not complete.

In some ways, God's revelation of himself to us is like that relay race. First, God revealed himself directly to men and women who were receptive to his voice, as he did to Adam and Eve, Enoch, Noah, Abraham, and Moses. Then, he had men like Moses pass the baton of knowledge of God to others by recording his revelation in writing, giving people the collection of books we know today as the Old Testament. The Old Testament pointed to the coming of Christ, and when he came, the baton of God's revelation to man was passed to him.

Jesus Christ carried the baton perfectly. He was the fullest revelation of God the world had seen since the fall of Adam and Eve. The apostle John called him "The Word," and that term tells us much about just how accurately he showed God to us. To illustrate what it means to call Christ the Word, consider all the ideas and thoughts that continually fill your mind. Those thoughts may be insightful and profound, but until you express them orally or in writing, they remain unknowable and invisible to others. When you embody those thoughts in words, they become tangible realities that others can apprehend with their senses.

That is what Jesus Christ did for the invisible God. He incarnated the mind, Spirit, and character of God in a body that we could apprehend with our senses. Just as words become the tangible expression of thought, Christ became the tangible expression of God. But unlike our words, which often fail to express our thoughts accurately, Christ articulated the nature of God perfectly. As Jesus often said in John's gospel, "The person who has seen me has seen the Father" (John 14:9).

How did Jesus manage to give us such a full and complete revelation of God? While on earth, he laid aside the prerogatives of power that belong to God and submitted his will to his Father's in heaven. He "learned to be obedient" as the writer of Hebrews tells us, and he told his disciples that he could "do only what he sees the Father doing" (John 5:19). He allowed God the Father to live in him, just as Adam and Eve before the fall allowed God's Spirit to live in them. And because Jesus was not tainted by the sin that dominates Adam's race, he could submit perfectly and allow God the Father to live in himself fully. For the first time since Adam and Eve fell, God had a man on earth who reflected his nature and his glory just as he intended from the beginning.

But after his crucifixion and resurrection, Jesus told his disciples that he could not stay with them. He had to return to his Father. Did this mean that God would no longer have a man on earth in whom he could live and reflect his nature? If that had been the case, the race would have been over. The baton would have been dropped with no one to carry it on the next lap. But look at what Jesus told his disciples just before he left: "I will ask the Father and he will give you another helper who will be with you forever. That helper is the Spirit of Truth" (John 14:16). Jesus had finished his lap of the race, and another runner was ready to take the baton.

A few days after Jesus returned to heaven, his disciples were together in a room celebrating the Jewish festival of Pentecost when suddenly flames of fire descended upon each of them, accompanied by the sound of a gale-force wind. Immediately, these men found themselves empowered to go out and speak to the huge crowd that had gathered to see what caused all the commotion. And speak they did. They told the story of Christ, and each disciple was able to speak in the language of whatever nationality of people had gathered around him.

With this astonishing miracle, the replacement Jesus had promised had come: the Holy Spirit of God descended from heaven to live within each of these disciples. They took the baton and became what Jesus was when he was on the earth—bearers of the life of God, reflecting his nature to the rest of creation.

Who Is the Holy Spirit?

Perhaps you have noticed that in every large organization, whether it's a business, a service club, a church, or a school, you often find one person who remains behind the scenes, always present but never prominent. He or she may seem insignificant— never on stage, never making speeches, never asserting authority or getting in the news. But more and more you realize that this person wields enormous power and influence, often equal to those who visibly run the show.

In some ways, this describes how the Bible presents the Holy Spirit. We know that all three persons of God were involved in creation, partly by the plural pronouns in the passage, "Let us make man in our image, in our likeness" (Genesis 1:26, NIV). The first chapter of John identifies Jesus, the second person of the Trinity, as one of those who made up the *us* and *our* in this verse. And the second verse of Genesis tells us that the Holy Spirit was also there, "hovering over the waters." He was involved in creation, though what he did remains a mystery. He stayed in the background as he does throughout the Bible. Though he is often mentioned, and evidences of his enormous power appear, as on the day of Pentecost, his words seem always to be spoken through others or revealed quietly to individuals. He is never identified as a distinct entity to whom we should specifically address devotion.

The Holy Spirit is the aspect of God that reaches out from him and enters those who are his own, helping them accomplish God's purpose. He strengthens, he gives courage, he brings new life, he protects, and he motivates toward right performance. He imparts to us the essence of himself, placing within our being the only power that can enable us to become more like God. As Paul tells us, the presence of the Holy Spirit is evidence backing up all of God's promises. "And when you believed in Christ, he identified you as his own by giving you the Holy Spirit, whom he promised long ago. The Spirit is God's guarantee that he will give us everything he promised" (Ephesians 1:13–14, NLT). His presence within us gives comfort that we are never alone. It gives us courage to stand against anything. And it gives our lives meaning in knowing we are fulfilling the role we are created to fill—to be God-bearers, displaying his nature to others who need to know him.

To many people today "the god inside each of us" means that we humans are really our own gods. They believe that we can find within our own resources the power to rise above our animal passions and achieve our own purposes.

Christians know better. God is truly a literal, personal, transcendent being separate from ourselves, and his Holy Spirit living within us is no mere figure of speech. The being who created the universe literally resides within our lives. If the god within is nothing more than one's own untapped resources, that person has no god at all.

The true God of the universe has given us himself. And this is not merely an abstraction or a metaphor. It is a literal reality. The actual person who created all worlds, who rules every atom in existence with a mighty hand, wants to come inside you in the form of his Holy Spirit and know you intimately, giving you all the comfort, courage, and assurance you need to live a life of joy and fulfillment.

The Spirit in Control

When we invite God's Spirit to enter our lives, does he completely take over, dominating our will and moving us about like puppets?

Not at all. God gave us the supreme compliment of freedom, allowing us to choose our own destiny and make our own decisions. That is the human dimension that separates us from the animals. Even when we submit to the direction of the Holy Spirit, that freedom is never taken from us. To remove it would violate our intrinsic nature as creatures of free choice and reduce us to something less than we were created to be. God does not override the freedom to choose that he gave us at creation.

The Holy Spirit provides the dynamic and motivating power for our lives, but that does not mean that God takes over and runs the show. It means that he nudges and prods us in the right direction. He draws us toward himself and provides power to accomplish his will when we choose to do it. But the decision to follow his will lies solely with us. Once we decide to act, his power kicks in, much like the power steering of your automobile kicks in when you turn it into your driveway. You decide to make the turn and provide the initial effort, and your effort activates a greater power that actually turns the car. You alone decide whether to run God's race, and when you make that decision, the Spirit will enable you with the strength and ability to do it.

Carrying the Baton

When we receive the Holy Spirit into our being and live as Jesus did, submitting our wills to God, we become replicas of Christ. We become what he was when he was on the earth—bearers of the life of God. We carry the baton into the next lap. But who is waiting for us at the end of our lap?

The Pentecost account in the second chapter of Acts shows us. Notice that after the disciples preached their sermons (only Peter's is recorded), three thousand people responded and were baptized, becoming Christians themselves. Do you see what happened here? These people who had never known of Christ saw and heard him reflected in these Spirit-filled disciples, and as a result, they became Christians as well. This means that God also gave them his Holy Spirit. In turn, they would go out and live their lives by the power of the Spirit, and others would respond and receive the Spirit. Thus the baton is passed again and again. The difference in the 400 meter relay and the race we run as Christians is that ours is not limited to four laps. It goes on and on until it reaches the finish line of eternity. Each of us who receives the Spirit of God must hand off the baton to the next runners. Since we are now what Christ was when he was on the earth—the embodiment of the Word—we are to do what Christ did: we make the invisible God visible to others.

Notice that with each revelation of himself, God moves closer and increases the intimacy of the relationship. In the Old Testament Scripture, he gave us words about himself—God *presented to* us. In Christ, he gave us a perfect reflection of himself—God *with* us. Then with the coming of the Holy Spirit, he places himself within the lives of Christians—God *in* us. Each step is closer and more intimate.

People today are often introduced to God in a similar way. First, they read about him in the Bible or hear about him through teachings or sermons (God presented to them). Then, they see him reflected in the lives of Christians (God shown to them). And finally, they invite him into their lives and come to know him personally (God experienced in them).

Passing the Baton to the Next Generation

God has given parents, grandparents, youth workers, and teachers an incredible honor and an awesome responsibility. He has made parents partners with him in populating eternity. He allows us to launch into existence beings capable of bearing the glory of God forever in a state of immense joy.

That little thumb sucker in your crib may have morphed into a baffling teenage creature dressed in outlandish outfits and operating from a mind tuned to an alien wavelength, but he or she has the capacity to become a magnificent being equaling the beauty and perfection of Adam or Eve. The problem is that this destiny is not automatic. Our children are born into our image, but they must be shaped into God's image. Just as God molded Adam from clay, he depends on us to participate in the molding of our children into his likeness. Our partnership with God is only beginning when our child is born. Our children are given to us so that we can give them back to God. Your child is to be made his child. The Israelites under Moses took this parental responsibility seriously. God told them to commit themselves to his commands and to be extra diligent in passing them on to their children. He admonished: "Repeat them again and again to your children. Talk about them when you are at home and when you are away on a journey, when you are lying down and when you are getting up again" (Deuteronomy 6:7, NLT). God was telling Hebrew parents that the one sure way to keep the reality of God alive in their children was to saturate their minds continually with the knowledge of him. They countered negative outside influences by making knowledge of God as much a part of their children's everyday existence as eating and breathing.

Not only parents, but any of us who have young people in our charge play an important role in the process of bringing today's kids to the knowledge of the God who can complete them. In fact, in this day of broken homes and harried single parents, our responsibility and opportunity is even greater. The duty of all of us who have young people in our environment is to convey to them the essence of what God is about with humankind—to show them that he is real and that he wants a relationship with them that will give life meaning and enfold them with love. The way to accomplish this is not merely to tell them—not just to load them up with instructions, data, admonitions, and propositions about the truth but, like the Israelites under Moses, to maintain a close relationship with them in order to show them experientially that God is real and relational. The only effective way to pass the baton is to allow his relationship with you to overflow into their lives.

In stressing the importance of relationship, we are not denying the importance of conveying facts. As we said in chapter one, it is crucial that our young people know that Christianity is factual. Without the knowledge that Christ really came down to us, the claim that God wants a relationship with us floats off into the realm of myth and wishful fantasy. The rational foundation of fact is essential.

But it is not in knowing the facts that we experience the joy of God. The rational mind knows, but it doesn't feel. And feelings are where we experience the joy that makes existence worthwhile. As Pascal said, "It is in the heart that we experience God." Yes, the rational mind must affirm the facts before the heart can act with confidence. But most people are won through the heart, not through the mind. Facts are needed, but it's the living demonstration of the truth that drives it home.

Our kids are not out there looking for knowledge; they are looking for experience. They're not banging on the doors of peer acceptance, sexual experimentation, drugs, and gangs in order to learn facts, but in a desperate search for firsthand experiences that will satisfy those driving needs for relationship. Those desires for love, understanding, acceptance, and stable relationships that so many of our young people seek in all the wrong places are actually God-given longings. God placed these desires in human hearts in order to draw us to him. Everything we desire and need is met in relationship with God.

Convincing our young people that Christ is historically real is necessary, but it is not enough to bring him alive in their lives. It's hard to pitch facts and make them meaningful across the chasm of their skepticism or indifference. That's why it is so important for adults to develop relationships with young people. Relationship provides an effective bridge. In relationship you expose them to the truth of God simply because God lives in your own life. And you can be sure that they will sit up and take notice.

When they see Christ demonstrated in your life, they will experience him in their relationship with you. You will not be merely telling, you will be demonstrating the truth of Christ's claims in an experiential way that affects them directly. We relate to them as God relates to us. We become conduits of his love, passing on what we receive from him just as a pitcher filled from a kitchen tap pours what it receives into glasses to be served. The adult-child relationship prepares the hearts of our children for a relationship with God by allowing them to experience it "second-hand" through their relationship with us. They come to know God as we reflect God's nature. We "act like God" to them.

Former church youth minister and author of the book, *Postmodern Youth Ministry*, Andy Harrington said it well in an article he wrote for *Youthworker Journal*. Though he was writing specifically to youth ministers, his advice is applicable to parents, grandparents, teachers, and any Christian involved in the lives of young people.

> This is how [our young people] see the truth, in lives lived out loud in which they can participate. It's a kind of relational osmosis that's custom built for the postmodern mind-set. Teens desperately need authentic role models that scream out the Jesus truth in every situation. Let their eyes see the truth in your life. Take the time for the one-on-ones, the invites home, the hanging out, and the friendship building. If that makes you feel uncomfortable, well, sorry; but that's the Jesus way. It's called love.[1]

I (Tom) was richly blessed in that my own father modeled this kind of love to me. Early in my life, for all practical purposes, Dad was God to me. His relationship to me was based on love, and his presence in my life fulfilled all my needs. But in time, I began to glimpse the reality behind my father. I began to see that he was a "middleman" between God and me. I began to see that the relationship he had with me was a replica of a relationship that he had with God. In his relationship with me, I glimpsed my first visible image of what God is like. My eyes traveled up the beam that reflected off him and saw the true source of the light that illuminated his life.

Whether you are a parent, grandparent, youth worker, teacher, mentor, school bus driver, coach or anyone involved in the life of young people, you can have an eternal impact on their lives and change their direction simply by modeling the nature of God to them in your relationships. In the following chapters of this book, we will outline basic principles and flesh them out with numerous illustrations to guide you in achieving this goal. We will give you solid handles by which you can identify and activate ways of relating to your young people in four areas that we have identified as being critically important to them. We are convinced that youth today are trying desperately to fill four basic needs in their lives:

- unconditional acceptance
- intimate understanding
- sacrificial love
- continuing relationship.

Happily, these four needs just happen to be those that a relationship with God fulfills in each one of us. In the next section, we will help you identify these needs in your young people and lead them into a fulfilling relationship with God.

PART II

Revealing God to the Next Generation

PART II

SECTION 1

God Understands Us Intimately

CHAPTER 4
Our Need for Intimate Understanding

Jason sat on his bed, staring at the floor. He could not believe what had just happened. Troy was his best friend, or so he had thought. They had been buddies since grade school. They had joined band together and had often stayed overnight in each other's homes, playing computer games, confiding their problems, their dreams, and of course, their thoughts about girls. Troy had always been interested in football, though he was not large enough to play. But when he had found that the equipment manager's position was open, he applied and got the job. That was when things began to change. Troy had to quit band to attend football practice, meaning that he and Jason spent less time together. But their friendship had remained intact, or so Jason thought.

But at lunch today something happened. Troy and Jason had always sat together while the popular football boys sat with the cheerleaders at a table across the lunchroom. Jason and Troy were carrying their trays to their usual table when Bart, the Mac truck-sized, all-district tackle, called out, "Hey Troy, come over here and sit with us."

"Sure, I will! Thanks." Without a word to Jason, Troy turned away and sat with the football squad, leaving Jason to eat lunch alone.

Jason tried hard not to let it get to him. After all, it was probably just a one-time thing. He didn't own Troy. His friend had a right to sit with someone else now and then. But still it hurt. And the worse was yet to come. Between fourth and fifth periods, the two friends met at their side-by-side lockers.

"Don't forget," Jason reminded Troy, "you're coming over tonight to play Madden football on my PlayStation."

At that moment, Bart's mountainous hulk loomed out of nowhere. He draped his meat-hook arm around Troy and said,

"My buddy and I have other plans tonight, don't we Troy? We're going to the big party over at Sheryl's place. Her parents are out of town, and you know what that means." He wiggled his eyebrows suggestively. "I'm afraid this boy doesn't have time for kids' games any more, right old buddy?"

"Right!" said Troy, giving Bart a high five as the monster turned and lumbered down the hall.

Jason came home that afternoon and told his mother not to set a plate for Troy that night. When she asked why, Jason blurted out the whole story. As usual, she responded with Scripture: "'Friendship with the world is enmity with God.' If that's the kind of friend Troy is, you're better off without him. There are plenty of good kids in the church youth group, and I've often wondered why you haven't made friends with one of them." Mom just didn't understand. A friend couldn't just be replaced like a battery in an iPod. She had no idea how much he hurt inside.

❖❖❖❖❖❖❖

As Wilson closed his Sunday school class of teenagers, he noticed that Kristin had not said a word the entire time. And she looked as if she were about to cry. Wilson knew something was wrong. The girl was usually bubbly and full of life, often answering his questions with unusual insight for one so young. As he dismissed the class and the kids left the room, he went over and sat in the chair beside her.

"Kristin, I don't want to pry, but I can't help but sense that something is wrong. Is there any way I can help you?" he said.

"Preston broke up with me," she wailed. "He has fallen in love with someone else." She buried her head in her hands and convulsed with sobs.

"There, there, it's not all that bad," he said. "At your age, it's only puppy love. Why, when I was a teenager, I fell in and out of love a dozen times a month. You are young, and you can't really know what love is yet. Besides, it won't hurt you to date other boys. You don't want to get serious until after you've completed your education. And since Preston was not a Christian, you are better off without him. You can date boys in the church here who will be much better for you."

Kristin just cried all the more. Why did adults always react this way? Had they never been young? Didn't they understand how badly it hurt to be rejected, especially to be replaced by someone else?

❖❖❖❖❖❖❖

Trevor, a high school senior, just made another *B*-minus in trigonometry, and again his father hit the ceiling. Trevor tried his best, but he just wasn't good in mathematical subjects. He was good at English, especially English literature, which he loved. He wanted to be a writer, but his father had lectured him again and again that most writers didn't make much money. He had insisted that his son take electives like trigonometry because they would look good on his college applications. If Trevor could keep up his grades, he could get into his dad's alma mater, earn a law degree, then join his father's firm, and in a few years become a partner. He would be set for life. Time and again, his father had told Trevor that he needed to give up this silly dream of being a writer. The John Grishams and J. K. Rowlings were rare. Most writers didn't earn enough to pay the rent on their one-room apartments. But his dad just didn't understand. The very idea of sitting in an office all day reading wordy legal documents and going over boring contracts depressed Trevor. He didn't want to be a lawyer like his father. Why couldn't his dad understand that?

The Longing for Understanding

Experiences similar to those of Jason, Kristin, and Trevor are being repeated all over America every day. Young people are experiencing pain, rejection, and fractured relationships, but they don't feel that the adults in their lives have a clue to what they are thinking or what they are going through. As they enter adolescence, they are discovering the power of that built-in desire that all humans have—the desire to be known, to be listened to, discovered, and affirmed for who they are as individuals. Adolescence brings inevitable feelings of insecurity as young people venture out of the safe haven of home and launch into the vast sea of outside relationships for validation of who they are. When these relationships hit the shoals, kids feel the hurt deeply. They are not accustomed to the power of the new emotions that assail them and don't yet know how to manage them. The pain feels too heavy to bear alone, and they desperately want someone to understand what they are going through and feel it with them. When they turn to adults, as Jason and Kristin did, they often don't get the kind of understanding they are seeking. Instead of finding understanding, Jason and Kristin found what they felt was condescension and instruction. The adults seemed to blow off the hurt as insignificant and get straight to the lesson to be learned. The pain was essentially dismissed as immature and unimportant in the larger scope of things.

When young people are feeling pain, the view from the larger scope of things is just what they don't want. They want to be seen not through the lens of expectations of conformity to a pattern, but as unique persons with individual desires, individual needs, and individual pains. Instead, they often feel that they are being viewed through a template. The template is a matrix of pre-scribed expectations that they must meet in order to earn approval. Wherever they turn, they encounter another list of expectations. At school, it's grades and behavior. In sports, it's following the rules and performing up to the level of the coach's demands. At church, it's obeying the Ten Commandments and behaving according to the moral code. At home, it's keeping Mom and Dad happy by meeting the expectations of all these other areas, plus the added expectations of doing chores and getting along amicably. They often come to feel that adults don't see them as real persons with individual needs but as cogs in various machines. When their needs—whether perceived or real—vary from the template, they feel misunderstood.

When kids come to feel that the adults in their lives don't understand them, they will turn elsewhere to satisfy their built-in desire for intimate understanding. They will typically gravitate toward peers who share the same kinds of problems. They will get understanding in the form of commiseration and develop a sort of bunker attitude toward adults, whom they think have lost touch with what it's like to have real feelings. And often with the support of such peers, they will embark on a search for ways to validate their desire for someone to know them intimately as persons by flouting the standards of their parents and adopting the values of their peers, engaging in peer activities such as drugs, alcohol, or seeking intimacy in sexual encounters.

As adults, we know that "templates" are not of themselves bad. An overarching standard to define behavioral expectations is necessary in a stable society. We need such a standard because we are fallen. Before Adam and Eve fell, no such pattern was needed. They were not infected with the tendency toward rebellion against rules that plagues us now. To them, good behavior was as natural as it is for salmon to swim upstream to spawn or geese to fly south for the winter. But now that we humans must contend with this fallen nature that continually pushes us toward selfish, socially-damaging behavior, we need the template. We need rules. We need those Ten Commandments to prescribe how to curb our sinful impulses and behave in a way that will maintain a stable society.

We adults know that these rules are not ultimately stifling; they are actually enabling. They make stable relationships possible. They allow us to live in a society free from constant fear of the unrestrained impulses of others. But to our young people just emerging into the awareness of selfhood, it seems the opposite. To them the rules seem to stifle individuality, to oppose self-realization, and to throw cold water on activities that look like great fun. When they come home hurt or want to try things potentially harmful and the first thing parents do is set the rules before them, they think they are not being seen as individuals. They feel they are being forced into the template of expectations.

The Lure of the Culture

The impulse toward independence rises up and comes on strong in adolescence. Young people are no longer content to live solely in the world of their parents. They peer out of the nest into the broader vista of the world outside and feel the urge to try their wings. This urge is natural and desirable, of course. But a critical problem in today's world is that this powerful impulse is amplified and egged on by advertising, movies, music, TV, teen magazines, and manufacturers of clothing, cosmetics, electronics, and automobiles, all of which have found a huge buying market in today's young, affluent generation.

And how do advertisers sell to this generation? Certainly not by appealing to the template of expectations. Dad and Mom already do that, and the kids resist it. Advertisers sell by appealing to our kids' vulnerabilities and insecurities. They find the desire and the weakness and exploit them. Kids are pulling away from Mom and Dad, trying to assert their personhood and find their individuality. So this is the button the media pushes. They egg on these budding impulses and insecurities. "Unsure that you fit in? Buy InThing brand of clothing like all your peers are wearing." "Unsure that you are attractive to boys? Use MaleMagnet makeup or Alluraroma perfume." "Do you feel that everyone (actually meaning Mom and Dad) is pushing you into a mold of conformity? Get wild. Color outside the lines. Assert your individuality. Be yourself. Do your own thing." Kids today are bombarded from every direction with the idea that living by the rules stifles individuality, and the way to be your own person is to resist the template.

So when Jason came home deeply hurt over being rejected by his best friend, his mother's immediate response of Scripture and admonitions didn't help. In fact, it only served to convince him that she did not understand. He was feeling deep emotional pain, and she was reminding him of the rules. Unwittingly, she was playing into the insecurities that the media had been enlarging and egging on in Jason's mind. "Your parents want to force you into a template. They don't understand your deepest needs. Only others like yourself can understand what you feel. You need to align yourself with other displaced young people and identify with them. You need to adopt their values, look like they do, play the same games, see the same movies, listen to the same music, read the same magazines, and buy the same clothes." What Jason needed from his mother at that moment was not a reminder of the rules but simple understanding of his pain. (We will show how this understanding looks in chapter six.)

Trevor's father had good intentions in pushing his son to follow his footsteps into a law partnership instead of letting him fly off into a dicey career in the field of writing. From his rational point of view, his goals for his son made perfect sense. He had a lucrative business already established and running—one that he had built from the ground up with his own hands. He expected his son to step in and take it over when he retired. But he did not understand his son intimately.

Of course we deplore postmodernism's disdain for absolutes, but postmodernism does have a positive side in its emphasis on relationships and a hunger for the spiritual. The present generation of young people is among the most idealistic of any to come along in a long while. The pendulum has, in some ways, swung away from the materialism of the previous generation. Many of the current crop of kids have seen the futility of acquisitiveness, so having it all does not appeal to them. Even the drive for financial security does not tempt them. They want to make a difference in this world and leave the stamp of their presence upon it. Trevor's choice of a career reflected this attitude, but his father couldn't see it. He looked at Trevor through the template of his own generation's values and Trevor did not fit, so he took steps to push his son into the template. He failed to see his son as a person in his own right with individual needs. He failed to understand his son, and his son knew it.

What will Jason, Kristin, and Trevor do in the face of adult failure to understand their innermost feelings? Their desire for intimate understanding is too strong to ignore. It is a real need, and it will not rest. As we have said, they will inevitably turn to their peers who share the same hurts and the same frustrations. In their mutual commiseration, they will adopt the views and outlook of each other, which they don't realize is really shaped by cultural influences. They will reject the template and assert their individuality with a vengeance. They will adopt the credo of the current generation (which is actually as old as the fall)— "Whatever you choose to do is right for you. No one has the right to tell you what to believe or what to do." Parents and all they stand for will become the enemy.

It is not unusual for young people to think no one understands them. At some point, it's the cry of every person entering adolescence in every generation. You probably said it yourself more than once in your teen years. But as we have shown, today's young people are much more vulnerable to outside forces when they utter that cry. The call of the culture is so pervasive and so strong that now perhaps as never before in history we in America are in danger of losing a generation of young people to the values of the culture. In the past, we have always been able to rely on the general religious consensus of society. Our nation was largely shaped and founded by men with a strong commitment to God as the authority for human government. And from the beginnings of the nation until the second half of the twentieth century, Christianity was the dominant religion. The majority of Americans either professed Christianity or accepted the presence of Christian-based principles in the outlook, morality, and conduct of everyday life.

But not any more. A seismic cultural shift has occurred, and we no longer have the culture on our side as we shape our young people. Christianity is no longer the dominant religion. While many still profess it, much of their belief has taken on a form that little resembles classical Christianity. As we have said, they see it not as *the* truth but as *a* truth. Not as the only true religion, but as one religion among many, all equally valid. Those who hold to the old view—that Christianity alone is true—have become targets for disdain and even hostility, and attacks have been launched against Christianity that are not tolerated against any other religious group.

Lured by a culture that is hostile to Christianity, the idea that our young people's craving to be understood could be satisfied in Christ never enters their heads. What has religion got to do with their need for intimate understanding? In their minds, the two ideas are not even linked. But as you know, their desire for intimate understanding is one that Christ only can satisfy and one that he longs to satisfy. He understands each of us intimately and perfectly like no one else can. Our young people misunderstand Christ largely because adults are not showing them the kind of intimate understanding that Christ offers.

We are convinced that when our young people thoroughly understand this central truth of Christianity, their lives will be revolutionized. They will no longer be adrift and thirsting for understanding on the chartless seas of insecurity. When it dawns on them that Christ is a real person who offers a real relationship characterized by an intimate understanding of their deepest needs, their fondest dreams, and their highest hopes, the culture will lose its appeal, and they will turn to him in droves.

In this chapter, we have merely set up the need. We have tried to show how strong and crucial is the longing in the human heart for intimate understanding. We have shown how well-meaning adults often fail to address the deep need for understanding when our kids cry out for it. And we have shown how the legitimate need for values and the illegitimate lure of the culture challenges our attempts to meet our kids' need for understanding. We are convinced that parents, youth workers, teachers, and others involved in the lives of youth are in a position to show their young people the truth of Christ as the ultimate relationship that will bring intimate understanding to their lives. In the next two chapters, we will explore the reality of Christ's ability to provide intimate understanding and give you practical steps to connect your young people to him.

CHAPTER 5

How Christ Meets Our Need for Intimate Understanding

To say that I did not have an ideal childhood is a gross understatement. My father was the town drunk. He beat my mother regularly, and serious family blowups were common. I don't know how many times deputy sheriffs had to come to our house to restore order. Everyone knew of my father's drinking and abusive behavior, and I was extremely embarrassed to be known as his son. I don't know how I would have gotten through childhood and adolescence had I not known that my mother understood my humiliation and hurt. But my mother was a broken woman. Shortly before I graduated from high school, I came home one night and found her crying. Thinking my father had beaten her again, I asked her what was wrong.

"I just can't take it anymore," she sobbed. "Your father . . . his drinking . . . his abuse. I've lost the will to live. I want to hang on until you graduate next month, then I just want to die."

I had heard her say such things before, but this time I sensed that she meant it. And she did. I graduated from high school, and a few months later my mother died. My father's cruelty had destroyed her will to live.

I was devastated. With the death of my mother, I lost the only person who ever seemed to understand me. She understood because she shared my world. She lived in the same dysfunctional and abusive environment. She knew firsthand what it was like to live in constant fear, anger, and embarrassment. No matter what I did, no matter where I went or how late I came home, she had always been there for me. But suddenly she was gone, and I felt that I had no one to turn to. No one else could possibly know what it was like to be me.

Of course I had friends at school, but they didn't understand me. How could they? They couldn't know what it was like to be the son of the town drunk. They all knew of my father's rampant alcoholism and made jokes about it. I joined in with their humor and added jokes of my own, and no doubt my friends thought it didn't bother me. But it did. I tried to cover up the hurt with the humor, but the hurt was there, eating away at me. How could I expect them to understand? They never experienced what I had gone through.

The Message of the Incarnation

Even after I became a Christian, I did not realize how Christ understood my pain. Yes, I knew that God loved me so much that he gave his Son to die for me, and I was deeply grateful. But for years I somehow missed the fact that the whole purpose of his coming was for a relationship. I failed to see the purpose of Christ's coming as a restoration of the intimacy with God that we had lost in Eden. I failed to see how his life on earth showed me that God knew what it was like to be human, to suffer and experience rejection and humiliation. At some point, that truth began to penetrate my skull, and I was elated to know that the God who created me understood my pain and wanted me to share it with him in an intimate relationship based on love.

God offers this kind of comfort to all those young people who think nobody understands them, and their number is legion. If we can get that message to penetrate their mistaken ideas about Christianity, it will divert them from the lure of the culture and bring them a sense of peace like they've never known before. But you may ask, "If kids are already convinced that parents and other adults don't understand them, why should they believe that God does? If they don't think people separated from them by only one or two generations understand them, how can we lead them to think the God of the ages who is off up there in heaven could possibly know what we mortals go through down here, much less what adolescents go through?"

We must show them that God knows what we go through because he experienced it all firsthand. Because Christ took on human form, we can know that he truly understands our pains, our sorrows, our temptations, and our rejections. Our minds are hardly big enough to grasp the enormity of this truth. Christ is the all-sufficient Master of the universe, yet he became as dependent as you were when you were an infant. He was the one who designed and formed the human body, yet like you he had to learn to walk. The apostle John tells us that he was the preexistent Word, the perfect expression of the nature of God (John 1:1–14). Yet he had to learn to talk just as you did. He created the molecular combination of hydrogen and oxygen that gives us water, yet he got thirsty and yearned for a drink just as you do. Though he was Lord of creation, he grew up as an obedient son, subjecting himself to the will of a human father that he himself created. He learned the trade of carpentry, working with muscle-powered first-century hammers and saws as sweat dripped into his eyes and calluses formed on his hands and feet. He endured the blistering sun as he erected beams and rafters in the dust and stifling heat of Palestine.

Why did the God of heaven leave his perfect home to endure all these humiliations as one of his creatures? Of course, we know the overarching answer: He came to die for us to save us from our sins. That is really all the reason we need, and if it were the totality of the truth, we should be content and grateful. But it does not explain why he lived on the earth as a human for a third of a century. As far as we know, perhaps Christ could have saved us with a weekend trip to the earth, stopping over just long enough to perform the needed sacrifice and then getting off of this messed-up planet as fast as he could, not sticking around to endure all the muck we humans have to sludge through. I once knew of a preacher who performed his job this way. He showed up on Sunday morning to preach, delivered an excellent and resounding sermon, and then immediately slipped out the back door until the next Sunday. He didn't hang around after services to greet the crowd, didn't mix with the members, and didn't get involved in their lives. He was hired to preach, and none of that other stuff was in his contract. Perhaps Christ could have done his job the same way, and we still would have been eternally grateful to him for saving us. But he did so much more. He spent a lifetime mixing with us, eating our food, enduring our problems, and experiencing our pains and our joys.

Christ chose to spend time with us for a reason that tells us more than words ever could about the intensity of God's love. The Bible tells us that he left the glories of heaven and, "He made himself nothing; he took the humble position of a slave and appeared in human form" (Philippians 2:7, NLT). Why did he do this? Not only to save us, but to let us know he understands us and identifies with us. "Because Jesus experienced temptation when he suffered, he is able to help others when they are being tempted" (Hebrews 2:18). His life on earth as a man assures us that he is one of us in every way. We are told that he "is able to sympathize with our weaknesses. He was tempted in every way that we are" (Hebrews 4:15).

At this point, another question may enter your mind. Did God actually have to experience being a human in order to know what it was like? Doesn't his omniscience mean that he knows all? Isn't his knowledge perfect and all-encompassing without having to resort to "trying it to see what it's like?"

Yes, no doubt Christ could have understood us perfectly without actually enduring the experience of being human. But would you have then known that he understands you? He wanted you to know without a doubt. He was not content just to tell us he understood; he chose to show us. He didn't just *say* he wanted a relationship with us; he came and engaged in relationships. He wanted us to know beyond question that he understands what we go through as humans. He wanted us to know that his understanding of us was not mere head knowledge; it was drawn from actual hard-earned experience. He demonstrated his identification with us by his intimate involvement in human life. He did not merely know our pain; he felt our pain.

As the author of our story, Christ knew the ending would be good. Yet when he came to live among us our trials and tragedies affected him deeply, even though he knew them to be temporary. It's one thing to say, "I feel your pain" (we've heard politicians say that and found it hardly believable), but what if you had actually seen Jesus cry because he felt your hurt? Wouldn't you know beyond all doubt that he really did understand? It happened. Jesus was returning to Bethany, and as he entered the town, people met him and told him that Lazarus had died four days prior. Jesus knew that he would soon raise his friend from the dead, but when Lazarus's sisters, Mary and Martha, led Jesus to the grave, sobbing as they walked, their grief moved him deeply. Overwhelmed by their sorrow, he broke down and cried (John 11:17–44). He knew that their pain was temporary, yet he identified with them completely because he saw death through human eyes and grieved because their sorrow touched his heart. He understood, and because of his tears, they knew it with a certainty that mere telling would never accomplish.

How We Know That Jesus Understands

Looking at the life of Jesus leaves no room for doubt that he understands what you are going through. Perhaps you have been rejected. You may have prepared yourself for a major promotion in your company only to be turned down and then see someone else take the position you dreamed of. Or worse, you may have worked with a company for years, thinking your position was secure until retirement, only to be caught in a budget-cutting layoff. Maybe a boyfriend or girlfriend has spurned you, one whom you thought cared deeply. Or maybe a husband or wife whom you thought loved you has divorced you. Jesus fully understands because he has been through it. He also was rejected.

When Jesus announced the beginning of his ministry in his hometown of Nazareth, the people he grew up with were deeply offended. "Who does he think he is, this upstart kid who used to work around the corner in his dad's carpentry shop?" In fact, they were so furious that they would have killed him had he not slipped away (Luke 4:14–30). His own brothers rejected him. They didn't believe in his ministry and taunted him about his so-called miracles (John 7:1–5). His heart was broken because he was rejected by the very nation God had prepared to bring him to the world. He looked out over the capital city and cried in anguish, "Jerusalem, Jerusalem, you kill the prophets and stone to death those sent to you! How often I wanted to gather your children together the way a hen gathers her chicks under her wings! But you were not willing" (Matthew 23:37).

Maybe you feel unloved because you have been abandoned. Perhaps your father left you when you were growing up and needed him desperately. Perhaps your wife or husband left you to raise a family alone. Or a trusted friend may have failed to be there when you needed him or her most. It happened to Jesus. At his hour of greatest need, when he was arrested and sent to the authorities, his twelve most trusted friends scattered and were nowhere to be found as he endured ridicule, torture, and a sham of a trial. The man who was considered his closest friend denied that he even knew Jesus (Matthew 26:69–75). And the most sobering rejection of all, that chilling cry from the cross, "My God, my God, why have you abandoned me?" tells us that in Christ's darkest hour even God had to turn his back on his Son (Mark 15:34). Jesus had taken on the unholy burden of our sins, and though it broke God's heart to do it, he had to reject our sins and the one who carried them in order to save us.

Perhaps you have been deeply misunderstood. Your attempts to help were interpreted as interference, your desire for peace as cowardice, or your refusal to compromise your deepest principles as rigid intolerance. Jesus was grossly misunderstood. His own followers often misunderstood him and began to fall away when his teachings got too close to home (John 6:66). Many misunderstood the purpose of his mission, thinking he had come to lead a rebellion against the Romans and reestablish Israel's independence. His hearers and his own disciples often had trouble grasping the truth of his message, confusing spiritual truths with physical realities (John 2:20; 3:4; 4:15, 31–34; 6:50–54; 8:22, 33–39).

Perhaps you have been betrayed. You may have shared confidences with a close friend you trusted only to find your words repeated in the ears of those who could use them to harm you. Perhaps you confessed a private sin to a trusted friend who betrayed your trust and told it to others. Perhaps you depended heavily on the confidentiality of a trusted a coworker who deliberately leaked information about your proposed product to a rival or a competitor. And you wonder if anyone understands why you are so hurt. Jesus understands. Judas, one of his own twelve apostles whom he called a friend, betrayed him to the authorities with a token of friendly greeting—a kiss (Matthew 26:47–49).

Maybe the misunderstanding you feel comes in the form of severe criticism. The harder you try to do the right thing, the more volatile the verbal barrage aimed at you. Perhaps you are at the point where you feel that you can do nothing right without someone coming down hard on you. Jesus also felt the pointed arrows of sharp criticism from the powerful religious leaders of his day. Looking at him through the lens of their self-righteous legalism, they found fault with everything he did and said. When Jesus mixed with notorious sinners and tax collectors to show them they were loved, the Pharisees snorted, "Why does [he] eat with such scum?" (Matthew 9:11, NLT). When they saw him picking a few heads of grain for a meager Sabbath lunch, they got huffy: "Your disciples shouldn't be doing that! It's against the law to work by harvesting grain on the Sabbath" (Matthew 12:2, NLT). They complained that Jesus didn't follow the traditional ceremonial washing of his hands before he ate (Matthew 15:2). When Jesus forgave a man's sins, they were outraged: "This is blasphemy! Who but God can forgive sins!" (Mark 2:7, NLT). Even when he performed the wonderful healing of the man who had been blind from birth, all his ice-hearted critics could see was that he had violated the law against working on the Sabbath (John 9:1–34).

Perhaps no experience of misunderstanding is more painful than when we are ridiculed. It can happen over small things or large. Perhaps you have suffered ridicule from a coworker for refusing to falsify a time card or pad an expense report. You may have suffered ridicule for refusing to watch a TV series you think is immoral or attend certain kinds of movies. Perhaps you have been ridiculed for your faith, asserting that the Bible is true and Christ is who he said he was. Even when you know you are right, ridicule makes you feel lonely. You feel that you are on the outside while everyone else seems to be in.

Ridicule is even harder on young people. Their peers can be incredibly cruel. Searching to find how they fit in, adolescents find security in conformity with each other. And when anyone gets out of step, the innate insecurity of the group triggers a defense mechanism in the form of ridicule. This ridicule can be cold-blooded. Kids are ridiculed for anything that makes them seem different—wearing the wrong shoes or the wrong brands of clothing, wearing glasses, being skinny, being heavy, having long legs or a long nose, having the wrong friends, pimples, using the wrong slang, refusing drugs, alcohol, sex, or tobacco, taking parents seriously, taking Christ seriously, or praying.

And what hurts young people most is that much of what they are ridiculed for they can do nothing about. They can't change their size; they must wear the clothes their family can afford; they can't help their need for glasses. Such ridicule can lead to despair because they desperately need someone to understand their pain and to love them and accept them for who they are—pimples, glasses, Wal-Mart jeans and all.

Jesus understands. Does he ever understand! He was ridiculed mercilessly during his arrest and trial. The Roman soldiers guarding him ridiculed his claim to be a king:

> They took off his clothes and put a bright red cape on him. They twisted some thorns into a crown, placed it on his head, and put a stick in his right hand. They knelt in front of him and made fun of him by saying, 'Long live the king of the Jews!' After they had spit on him, they took the stick and kept hitting him on the head with it (Matthew 27:28–31). They blindfolded him and said to him, 'Tell us who hit you.' They also insulted him in many other ways (Luke 22:64–65). As Jesus hung on the cross, naked, bleeding, and in agony, those who saw him said, 'Save yourself! If you're the Son of God, come down from the cross.' The chief priests together with the scribes and the leaders made fun of him in the same way. They said, 'He saved others, but he can't save himself. So he's Israel's king! Let him come down from the cross now, and we'll believe him. He trusted God. Let God rescue him now if he wants. After all, this man said, "I am the Son of God." Even the criminals crucified with him were insulting him the same way' (Matthew 27:40–44). The soldiers also made fun of him. They would go up to him, offer him some vinegar, and say, 'If you're the king of the Jews, save yourself!' (Luke 23:36).

I suppose the reason I joked along with my friends about my dad's drunken behavior was to deflect their ridicule. If I could show that I identified with them instead of with my father, they would not ridicule me for being the son of such a despicable man. I was sure they would not understand my real feelings, which were deep humiliation and hurt. I was sure that nobody could really understand the pain of having everyone look at me and know that I was the son of the town drunk. So I covered up my feelings and joined in the ridicule of him to keep it from hurting me.

Even after I became a Christian I bore the hurt alone, feeling this permanent humiliation inside that I kept bottled up in fear of people's reaction. Later I found that it was not necessary for me to bear this fear. As I learned more about who Christ was, I realized that he had been through an experience quite similar to mine. Because of the unique and miraculous circumstances of his birth, people knew that his mother Mary was pregnant before she married Joseph. Naturally, people did not understand the real truth, and we can be sure that they talked behind the backs of the family and probably sometimes to their faces. We know that the stigma of illegitimate birth followed Jesus into adulthood because John records a taunt by some of the leaders opposing Jesus (John 8:41). We can be virtually certain that all his life he bore the stigma of suspected illegitimacy. So, could I continue to claim that no one understood my humiliation about my parentage? No. I knew that Jesus understood exactly what I was going through. He had been there.

Of course, Jesus did not merely experience the low points of human existence. He also knew what it was like to be loved and accepted. Joseph and Mary loved him and accepted him fully as a son in spite of his divine origins. He knew the joy of fulfilling his heavenly Father's will, and it must have delighted him to hear the voice of his Father say, "This is my beloved Son, and I am fully pleased with him" (Matthew 17:5, NLT). In spite of their human weaknesses and lapses, his disciples—except for one— were thoroughly dedicated to him. He had other friends as well, such as Mary, Martha, and Lazarus, who would do anything for him. He understood the joys of human friendship and human love.

Jesus also experienced human achievement and victories. No doubt he felt a sense of pleasure at completing a well-crafted table. He delighted when people responded positively to him in faith. He successfully trained twelve men who went out and changed the world. And he experienced final victory over what had never before been conquered—death.

Christ, the Word made flesh, shows us that he knows all about what it's like to be human, both the ups and the downs. But it seems that it's in the downs that we feel most acutely our need for understanding. The problem of suffering and pain is a perennial question in the minds of many skeptics, seekers, and Christians as well. The problem has excellent and understandable answers, and questions about grief and suffering need not trip up anyone who finds them to be obstacles to the truth of Christianity. But while the intellectual apologetics for pain are valid and powerful, perhaps none of them have the impact of this simple fact: No matter what you have to endure, no matter what you are feeling, and no matter how debilitating your grief, God did not leave you to suffer through it alone. He came down and got in this messed-up world with us. His message is, "I know that while you are experiencing the debilitating pain of this moment, rational explanations won't help. You don't need assurance that it will pass. You don't need to hear that there is hope tomorrow. You don't need to hear that every cloud has a silver lining. You simply need someone to understand. I *understand*. I know what you are going through. I am in this with you because I love you. I will not leave you to endure it alone."

This is the message of the God who became one of us.

CHAPTER 6

Modeling Intimate Understanding

Felicia got off the school bus and walked slowly up the sidewalk to her front door. She entered and went immediately to the kitchen where her mother was preparing dinner.

"Hi, Mom," she said, trying to sound cheerful as she dropped her backpack and sagged into a chair. But her mother could hear signs of dejection in Felicia's voice, and she knew that something was wrong.

"Hello, Felicia," she replied, lifting her flour-whitened hands out of the batter she had been mixing. "Is everything OK?"

"We had tryouts for the senior play today, and I didn't get the part." Felicia's voice quavered and tears welled up in her eyes.

"Oh, I'm so sorry, Felicia. I know how disappointed you must be. You worked so hard on your lines." Her mother quickly scrubbed her hands under the kitchen faucet.

"I just don't understand," said Felicia. "I tried so hard, and I prayed hard that I would get the lead role. But I didn't get that part or any other part. Mrs. Whittaker put me in the chorus again, just like last year."

"I know that really hurts," her mother replied as she dried her hands. "I can only imagine how you must feel. I hate it when you hurt like this. You know that God understands, too, don't you?" She threw the towel aside and walked around the table toward her distraught daughter.

"I know he does, Mom. You and Dad have told me that he understands all my hurts and troubles. And I guess I believe it. But . . . but—I don't know whether it's OK to say this—but sometimes that just doesn't seem to be enough. I know God loves me, but I can't see him. I know I can talk to him, but it would be nice to hear a real voice answering back. It helps in a way to know that he understands, but I just need someone I can see and feel and discuss things with. I can't hug God—do you know what I mean? It would help if God could hug me right now."

"I understand exactly how you feel," said her mother as she sat in the chair beside her daughter and enfolded the girl in her arms. "I feel the same way, and God does too. God wants to hug you. In fact, he's hugging you right now. He does a lot of hugging, but he does it through all the people who love you—your father, your sisters, Granddad, and me. He is in us, and he is using my arms to hug you at this very moment." She squeezed her daughter lovingly. "Felicia, I love you so much, and I always will. Whether you are the star of the play or not, you are the star of my heart. But it hurts me to see you hurt. I wish I could just hug away the pain."

"Actually, you're doing a pretty good job of it, Mom," said Felicia, laughing in spite of herself.

Felicia was making a good point when she said she needed someone to hug. The phrase we often hear, "Jesus is all you need," is the truth as far as it goes, but it's not quite an accurate way of stating the whole truth. God is the ultimate fulfillment of all our needs, but he never intended to be the only entity in our environment. When he created Adam, he allowed this first man to exist for a short while without Eve. Adam had God for companionship and a forest full of delightful animals for company, but God knew it was not enough. "It is not good for the man to be alone," he said (Genesis 2:18). Humans need other humans. They need the companionship of their own kind because God created this need within them. He created us to live in community with each other. The apostle Paul tells us that "we are joined together in his body" (Colossians 2:19, NLT).

Because Adam needed human companionship, God gave him Eve. Eve was not created to be a replacement for God. The companionship between the first couple was not meant to exclude him. He was to be an integral part of the relationship. His Spirit lived inside the man and woman, which meant that when they were in community with each other, they were also in community with him. In fact, Adam and Eve displayed God to each other. Adam experienced God in Eve; Eve experienced God in Adam. When they embraced each other, God was loving them and being loved by them. God intended for this loving community to expand as Adam and Eve loved into existence little copies of themselves. In reproducing, they would expand the community of love. They would create new little God-carriers who would also be filled with the Spirit of God and love others with his love. The interactive community of God and humanity would fill the entire earth.

But as we explained in chapter two, these first two humans rejected the Spirit of God in their lives, and no human after them displayed the nature of God perfectly until Christ came in subjection to the will of the Father and allowed God's Spirit to live in him, displaying God's love and understanding to all creation. When Christ ascended to heaven after his resurrection, God's Holy Spirit came down to live in the bodies of Christians just as God had lived in the body of Christ. Christians have been aptly called the "second incarnation," meaning that we duplicate the function of Jesus when he was on the earth. Just as God entered a human body in the incarnation of Christ, God now enters the body of every Christian, all of whom collectively form the body of Christ, called the church. As the apostle Paul tells us, "Even though we are many individuals, Christ makes us one body and individuals who are connected to each other" (Romans 12:5).

We take God into our lives and display his nature to each other. We experience God in each other. We pass on God's love. We model his love by loving others the same way he loves us, and others model him to us. We "distribute" God's love and understanding. What this means in practical terms is that when anyone feels disconnected, alone, rejected, or devastated by illness or grief, other members of the body should rally to that person and supply whatever is needed—connection, company, acceptance, understanding, or comfort.

After Felicia had failed to get a part in the play, she felt rejected and needed understanding and affirmation that she still had value and was worth loving. Her mother supplied it beautifully. But in reality, God supplied it beautifully. Through her mother, Felicia received God's love and comfort in a tangible, audible, huggable human form. Her mother did for her exactly what Christ did for hurting people when he was on earth. She showed God's love and understanding, and by doing it, she displayed the love of Christ.

When you reach out and connect with a young person, the Spirit of Christ actually ministers through you to that person. We are not merely offering our own care; we function as a conduit for God's care. This reflecting the image of God is, and has always been, the essence of the Christian life (Matthew 25:31–40). Today it is doubly important that our young people see Christ in us because the culture relentlessly pulls them away from all things Christian. We win them by showing them God in our being in a way that no indoctrination, no sermonizing, no theological apologetics can. We win them by displaying the winsome nature of Christ in our own lives. Each of us can become a walking, relational apologetic for the truth of Christianity.

Modeling Intimate Understanding to Young People

The key to showing your young people that you understand them is to give them a sense of authenticity. Many of them think we don't understand them as individuals. They think we look at them as projects to be molded to fit a template of expectations. Many of them think we don't respect them as fully authentic humans in their own right but that we treat them broadly as a sort of subclass of humanity. No adult does this deliberately, but sometimes, we may do it unintentionally even from the best of motives.

- Melissa's mother has opened all her daughter's personal mail ever since a boy she once dated sent her a steamy letter filled with suggestive language.

- When Jeremy is out for the evening, his father occasionally comes into his son's room and searches all the drawers and closets for drugs. He has no reason to suspect Jeremy, but he is highly concerned about teen drug use and wants to be sure his son is not involved.

- Angela's mother never knocks before entering her daughter's room, even though Angela is now fifteen and wants privacy. "Mom! I'm not dressed!" the girl screamed when her mother walked in unexpectedly after her bath. "Oh, don't be silly," the mother responded. "I'm your mother. I've changed your diapers a thousand times."

Some parents may think such treatment of young people is acceptable or in some cases necessary for their protection. Perhaps if Jeremy's father had good reason to suspect Jeremy was doing drugs, his investigations of his son's room might be justified. But if we followed the golden rule with our young people as we do in other relationships, we would never think of violating their personhood with such invasions of their space without compelling, overriding reasons. Kids will naturally draw away from close relationships with adults who do not give them basic respect as persons. Such treatment is even likely to trigger outright rebellion. Consequently, intimate understanding between adults and kids will be impossible until adults affirm young people's authenticity.

Another common barrier to intimate understanding between adults and young people is our kids' perception that often adults don't really listen to them when they unload their hurts and disappointments. This perception is reinforced when adults use the occasion for blame or as a reminder that the young person brought the problem on himself by failing to act wisely or according to adult advice:

"If you'd listened to me you wouldn't be in this mess."

"You've made your bed, now lie in it."

"Don't come crying to me. You knew better than to do that."

Predictable stock phrases such as these do nothing to motivate the young person toward better behavior. On the contrary, young people are likely to draw away from opening their hearts to adults who give them such responses. Words like these do not signal intimate understanding of their hurts and needs. In fact, the kid is likely to interpret such responses as rejection.

Parents and youth workers often address kids' problems with another kind of response that is meant well as a sincere attempt at encouragement. At the Friday night youth rally, the youth pastor noticed that sixteen-year-old Jessica seemed to have a cloud of gloom hanging over her head. He took her aside and asked what was wrong. "I lost my job today," said Jessica, dejection dripping from every syllable. "Cheer up, you'll find another," said the pastor. "The Bible says that all things work together for good, so hang in there. Everyone faces trials in this world, but you can pull through with God's help." This response was well meant to encourage Jessica, but it did not address her pain. She was hurting emotionally, and she needed someone just to understand the hurt and feel it with her.

The youth minister could have given her comfort by assessing how she felt. She had just lost her job, so she felt rejected, even if she was simply laid off in a corporate downsize that was no fault of her own. She may have felt angry or bitter toward her former employer, worried that her source of spending money was cut off, and fearful that she might not find another job. No doubt the youth minister had felt similar rejections, losses, and fears. He could draw on these experiences to place himself in Jessica's shoes and identify with her feelings. Then he would be ready to be a channel of comfort from God to her. His comfort might sound something like this: "Jessica, I am really sorry that you lost your job. I know you feel awful right now. It hurts me to see you hurting so much." Such kind, heartfelt words are sure to strengthen the connecting bond between young people and their caregivers.

Hear the Hurt By Listening to the Heart

The response that promotes relationship and shows intimate understanding is simply to listen, not merely to the problem, but to the heart. Hear the hurt behind the words and respond to the hurt.

This is what Felicia's mother did when her daughter was hurting from the rejection she felt at not getting the coveted part in the senior play. What the girl needed was a simple show of empathy, an indication that someone understood the hurt and felt it with her. When Felicia's mother said, "Oh, Felicia, I'm so sorry," and simply hugged her daughter, she was performing intimate understanding as Jesus modeled it. She did exactly as Jesus did. She first affirmed her daughter's authenticity as a person by understanding her feelings, regardless of the cause. She could have tried to put a "Christian" perspective on Felicia's disappointment: "Oh well, it's just a play, and in the larger scheme of things, it's really not that important. What's really important is your relationship with God." Had her mother responded in this way, Felicia would have felt that she was not being heard, that her mother saw her pain as frivolous, and failure to get a role in a play was beneath the level of proper Christian concern. She would have interpreted such a response as a mild reprimand and would have felt that her mother just didn't really understand.

At Lazarus' grave, Jesus did not say to Mary and Martha, "Your weeping is really unnecessary, so dry those tears. I'm going to take care of your problem," even though it was the truth. Instead, he broke down and cried, too. He understood their pain and felt it with them, no matter that the pain was unnecessary. The cause of the pain was unimportant to him at the moment. The fact that they were hurting touched him, and he affirmed the authenticity of their human feelings. He looked beyond the problem and saw the hurt. He understood their pain and showed it by weeping with them.

Providing a Comfort Zone

When a child falls and scrapes her knee, she runs crying to her mom or dad. Why? First for comfort, and then for a bandage. Even if the hurt is minor, children crave the comforting touch and words of a caring adult. That basic need doesn't change as kids grow older. Kids—and even adults for that matter—never outgrow the need to be comforted when they experience physical or emotional pain. Of course, we no longer climb up on someone's lap and ask them to kiss our owies, but we want someone to run to who we know will understand our pain. Our young people will learn to trust us and keep coming back if we provide understanding and comfort. They will see us as a safe haven where they can unload their cargo of cares.

When young people come to you with their deep hurts, they are not looking for a pep talk. ("Hang in there. When the going gets tough, the tough get going.") They are not seeking a theological treatise on why bad things happen to good people. They are not even looking for an analytical solution to their problem. First and foremost, they just want comfort. They want someone to understand that they have feelings in need of attention. They want somebody who cares to be there to listen. They want someone who will try to understand and identify with their feelings, not condemn them for having them. This doesn't always have to mean literal understanding. We can't always know exactly what they are going through. Some of their deep traumas may indeed seem frivolous to us. They may face emotional devastation over losing a football game, being turned down for a date, having a fender bender, getting a *C* on a report card, or breaking up with a boyfriend or girlfriend.

I (Tom) remember my first girlfriend breaking up with me when I was fourteen years old. My heart was broken, and I was devastated. I lost sleep pining and agonizing over her. For days I could think of nothing else. Wasn't it merely puppy love? Sure. Did I really know what love was about? No. Would it have helped me to hear this from my parents or youth minister? Absolutely not! At least, not while I thought my world had come to an end. The love I lost may have been shallow, but the pain of losing it was deep and real. It hurt. My youth minister could have responded, "Oh, get over it" or "If this is the worst you ever have to face, count yourself lucky" or "You are too young to really know what love is all about" or "Didn't I warn you about her? Breaking off is the best thing that could have happened. Count your blessings!" If he had responded with any of these profound gems of wisdom, would I have felt that he understood what I was going through? Hardly. Would I ever have shared my feelings with him again? Not a chance.

Such incidents may seem minor to us—just part of growing up—but they can be earth-shattering tragedies to our kids, and we must understand that. We must empathize with their pain. We must hurt with them.

When your kids confide their heartfelt emotions to you, if your first act is to point out the reality of the situation, correct the behavior, fix the problem, enforce the rules, chide them for inappropriate feelings, or treat the problem as trivial, you weaken your connection and push them away from the relationship. This kind of response makes the young person think you do not understand the depth of the need or the strength of the desire that led to the problem. Your interest seems to be in fitting him or her to the template, which means squashing the feelings, correcting the behavior, and ignoring or stifling the drive that led to it.

Instead, our first course of action should be to take the comfort of Christ to them when they hurt. The apostle Paul tells us that "he comforts us whenever we suffer. That is why whenever other people suffer, we are able to comfort them by using the same comfort we have received from God" (2 Corinthians 1:4).

"But these are our kids," you say. "They need help in fixing problems, and it's our job as responsible adults to provide it." True, but if we want to be effective, we will start from the other end. These are our kids, but first they are human beings created in God's image. They need the same kind of love that God has shown to us.

As we have been showing with examples from the life of Christ, love starts with understanding. To convince young people that you love them for who they are and don't see them merely as projects, you must genuinely enter into their feelings. You must know their heart. Deal with their feelings before you deal with the issues. Then you earn the relational position you need to correct the behavior, fix the problem, or enforce the rules. True, heartfelt, intimate understanding affirms their authenticity by taking their feelings seriously, thus strengthening the relational connection and making them willing to open up to you with their feelings and problems.

My son, Sean, played high school basketball. I attended one of the games and watched in pain as the coach verbally dressed down Sean in a big way. The man yelled and ranted at the poor boy, and even from the grandstand, I could see that Sean was deeply hurt. When he came home that night, I put my arm around him and said, "That must have hurt you badly when the coach got onto you tonight, right?" He nodded, too dejected to speak. "Sean," I replied. "I know that no one works harder at basketball than you. I truly hurt for you tonight, and I still do." It was clear that we really connected over the incident, and it seemed that my comfort helped him.

Later that week, I asked Sean's permission to talk to the school administration about the coach's hard-handed tactics. (He habitually treated other players the same way.) "You would do that for me?" Sean responded in amazement. "Sure, go ahead." So I made an appointment and confronted the coach in front of the school superintendent and athletic director, explaining how he was demoralizing Sean and the other boys on the team. The school dealt with the issue and completely resolved the problem. Sean was deeply touched that I affirmed his feelings and then dealt with his problem.

The hurt your kids feel must be separated from the source of the hurt, and we must deal with the two things separately. A key to a loving bond with your young person is to deal with the feelings before you deal with the problem. I had to deal with Sean's wounded spirit before I addressed its cause.

Affirming without Approving

The last bell had rung, and Kevin walked with his friend Ashton toward the parking lot. "Man, don't you let on to my parents that I got caught smoking in gym today," said Kevin. "I'll be in big trouble if they find out."

"Aren't you going to tell them?" asked Ashton.

"Are you crazy?" Kevin responded. "No, I'm not going to tell them! They would kill me. Surely, you don't tell your parents everything you do."

"Just about everything," replied Ashton. "Somehow they always seem to understand. They don't always approve, and sometimes they ground me or enforce some rules, but they always seem to understand. And that makes it easier to talk to them when I really have a big problem."

The tendency of many adults is to be more like Kevin's parents and blow up in anger over their kid's misbehavior. But such a negative reaction drives a wedge into the relationship. It says you don't understand their feelings or the need that drove them into the problem they're experiencing.

How do we convince our kids that we understand them without approving their wrong behavior? Often, they really do need correction. We have mentioned their resistance to being fitted to a template, but of course, we all know that there really is a template. We do have Ten Commandments that give us rules for moral behavior, and we must conform to these and other rules and teach our kids their importance. We can't approve their behavior when it is wrong, but it seems difficult for many of us to show our kids that we understand them and affirm their feelings without conveying the idea that we approve their behavior.

We can learn to separate feelings from behavior by looking at how Christ treats us. When you and I mess up, God loves us and addresses our needs even though we are wrong. When the Samaritan in Jesus' parable came upon the beaten man by the side of the road, he did not first ask, "Was this your fault? Did you deserve this beating? Were you the robber or the victim? Are you sure you took all the proper precautions against assault and robbery?" Instead, he felt compassion for the wounded man and did all he could to relieve his suffering. Jesus concluded the story by telling his listeners, "Go and imitate his example" (Luke 10:30–37).

So what if the pain is your young person's own fault—the consequence of ignoring God's provision or violating his law? Pain is still pain, and "pain hurts" as the bumper sticker says. It doesn't matter whether it is self-inflicted or inflicted by others. And all our pains touch the heart of God. To reflect the love of God, we must love our young people in such a way that their pain touches our hearts as our pains touch God's. We must first understand their hurt and deal with that, then address the deeper need. We do this by entering into their hearts to understand why they did what they did. Look for the need that drove the behavior and understand that need without affirming the behavior. "I understand why you went to that drinking party at Rick's house. 'Everyone else was going' and you wanted to be accepted. I know just how you feel. I often feel that way myself." Then from that platform of understanding you go on to show the better way to satisfy the need. By identifying with their hurts and recognizing their needs we show them that we understand. We take them seriously for who they really are—authentic human beings with real feelings and desires. With that kind of love and empathy firmly established, we can move to provide rules for future behavior in similar situations and even apply penalties for violating the rules. Once understanding is clearly established, the rules and penalties will be better accepted.

John 8:3–11 tells of the Pharisees bringing to Jesus a woman caught in the act of adultery. This woman's accusers were eager to condemn her, but Jesus saw more in her than just her guilt. He understood her heart. He understood whatever deep need she had that drove her to seek solace in the wrong man's arms. Though the behavior was wrong, the need was real; but it required redirection. Though she needed to change her behavior, Jesus knew that she did not need a sermon. She did not need condemnation, punishment, or a lecture. Christ showed her that she was understood as an authentic individual of immense value who was worth redeeming. After saving her from her self-righteous accusers, his words of admonition were simple but effective: "From now on don't sin."

Christ ministered to people even when the pain was their own fault. He earned the right to teach and correct by showing the depth of his care and demonstrating his understanding of people's needs. From this platform, what he taught "took" in their lives.

Understanding and Affirming

Understanding and affirming our young people starts with listening to them. The advice of the early church leader James is especially fitting: "Everyone should be quick to listen, slow to speak, and should not get angry easily" (James 1:19). When we listen as our kids share their feelings, we are saying to them, "I'm interested in you. I want to know how you feel. I want to know what makes you happy and what makes you sad. You are important to me." It's good to make listening a habit, not just something you do when problems arise. Stay involved in their lives so that the lines of communication are established and free of rust when they are sorely needed. Teachers can find a moment to sit down with a student and say simply, "Hey, I heard you won the debating contest," then really listen with interest as the kid recounts her triumph.

Meals are generally excellent times for parents to chat with their kids about their thoughts, feelings, and dreams. Parents should strive to keep meals upbeat and happy times for family bonding. They are not good settings for heavy instruction, correction, or criticism. The evening meal is a good time for family members to come together and communicate what has been going on in their separate lives during the day. When my wife and I (Tom) were raising our daughters, these daily family gatherings often extended past the eating itself. As we enjoyed each other's company, conversation ranged from important concerns to giggly silliness.

Youth workers often find that relationships blossom when they chat with students over a slice of pizza or an ice cream sundae. Young people are usually more open to conversation during a meal. If you can get them to talk about the day's events, their feelings will likely rise to the surface, giving caring adults opportunities to listen with concern and without reprimands.

Often you may find that the act of listening is virtually all that is needed. My wife Dottie once had a situation in which a woman poured out a deep hurt she was enduring. Dottie listened intently, occasionally putting in a word of caring interest. When the woman finished, she said, "I cannot express to you how much you have helped me today. I see my problem much more clearly. Thanks to you, I have a handle on it now." Dottie had hardly said a word the whole time but had simply listened sympathetically. You will be amazed at how just listening attentively and with a compassionate heart will help your kids feel understood and affirmed as valued individuals.

Of course, listening is merely one way of showing our young people that we understand them and affirm their value. Sensitive adults will adopt a habit of affirmation in which they maintain an acute sense of God's presence within themselves that reaches out and reflexively loves others. We have emphasized understanding young people when they experience problems because these are the times when the need is most obvious. But we also need to understand their triumphs as well. It's easy for busy people to slip into a habit of overlooking their young people's victories. The apostle Paul reminds us to enter into both the sorrows and the joys of others. "Be happy with those who are happy. Be sad with those who are sad" (Romans 12:15). When a daughter comes home with her first straight-A report card, she needs you to do a little more than glance up from the TV and mutter, "That's nice." You don't have to break out the champagne, kill the fatted calf, and call the local newspaper (even though you may consider such a rare event highly newsworthy), but stopping your routine and showing genuine pleasure in her triumph is appropriate. When your son catches the winning touchdown pass, he's going to come home that night with his feet hardly touching the ground. Wait up for him and recount the play a couple of times, telling him how you felt when he caught the ball and carried it across the goal line.

Sometimes, it's enough to affirm their excitement with comments like, "I am so delighted that this has happened for you" or "You have every reason to be thrilled. So am I." Sometimes you may feel that these rejoicing times call for celebrations or gifts. They need not be extravagant. Take the young person out for ice cream; buy him or her a new CD; allow a special privilege; or send an encouraging card. If you share their happiness by rejoicing with them, they will feel validated, and you will solidify the loving bond between you.

Later in this book, we will address the problem that can come from affirming kids only on the basis of performance, but this is not the same at all. What we are saying now is simply what we have been saying all along in this chapter—that you should empathize with their feelings—feelings of joy and elation as well as their lows. This kind of total understanding and positive involvement in their lives keeps the channels of communication intact and keeps your young people relationally connected to you.

We adults need to affirm our kids' good intentions. My (Tom's) wife Faye always encouraged our daughters' attempts to help her in the kitchen even when it would be much easier to cook the meal herself. She endured their awkward attempts at help with patience and without a hint that they were more in the way than helpful, thereby affirming their value by understanding their need to do something for their mother.

One July Saturday when I (Tom) was halfway through mowing my three-quarter-acre lawn, I took a short break to get a long, deep drink from the garden hose. After I had almost depleted the city water supply, I restarted the mower to continue. Moments later my seven-year-old daughter Jennifer came out of the house, smiling broadly and walking toward me clutching in both little hands a huge glass of cold water. I could have continued mowing and waved her off, saying, "Sorry, Jennifer, I just got a drink, and I can't possibly hold another drop. But thanks anyway." Can you imagine how she would have felt? She would have felt unimportant, unvalued, and that her efforts were unworthy and counted for nothing.

I stopped the mower, took the drink, gulped it down as if I had just crawled across the Sahara desert, and said, "Ahhh, thank you very much, Jennifer. That was really refreshing" as her happy blue eyes beamed with pleasure. I understood that she was not merely bringing water to me; she was bringing love. And there was no way I would fail to affirm that precious gift, no matter how much I sloshed inside as I continued my mowing.

Passing on the flame

The way God loves us is our model for loving others. Following his model of entering into the feelings of others to understand before we correct accomplishes two things: it improves our own relationships, and it reflects the nature of God.

To some people, the reflection of God in you may be the first, best, or only picture of him they have seen. Many people tend to form an image of God that is shaped by the distorted lens of their personal experience. For many the character of their own human father forms their first image of God. Your father may have been an overbearing, authoritarian figure, or perhaps he was distant, absent, or even abusive. You may have trouble thinking God understands you because your own father never understood you. By loving our kids and understanding them as God loves and understands us, we can do much to correct these false images of God formed through less-than-ideal or dysfunctional relationships.

Because so many families today are disjointed, distant, or dysfunctional, it's all the more important for those of us who deal with young people to form strong, positive relationships to show them the true nature of God. When you are in the company of young people, think of yourself as being a "little Christ" to them, showing by your own love and behavior what he is like. Just as God in Christ showed the world the nature of his love and how intimately he wanted to connect with us, let God's Holy Spirit in you show the nature of his love to your kids, so they will know how much he wants to connect with them and understand them intimately. And through you, they will learn to connect with God.

When You Must Stand Alone

Of course, we must remember that human relationship is not the only way to experience God. Occasionally God's people find themselves in positions where they must stand alone, utterly without human support or encouragement. And in those times, "Jesus is all you need" is the truth. He is truly there even when no one else is, and when you are dependent on him, you will find the support you need to get through the difficulty. Like Joseph, when you find no comfort from other people at all, and everything seems to be going against you, God is still there, and you can rely on him as the true source of strength and comfort. Though you can't see him, knowing he is there and that he cares will give you a sense of well-being.

Yet as we have shown in this section, God means for us to experience him through each other. And he depends on each of us to be God-carriers today just as Adam and Eve were created to be God-carriers in the beginning. With him living in us, our primary function as humans is to show his nature to the rest of creation and to demonstrate his love and intimate understanding in all of our relationships.

PART II

SECTION 2

God Accepts Us Unconditionally

CHAPTER 7
Our Need for Unconditional Acceptance

Corey tried not to show it, but he was dying inside. He stood with two other boys yet to be chosen for the two baseball teams in PE class.

"Kent," called out one of the team captains, and Kent stepped over to stand with the blue team.

"Tyler," called the captain of the red team, and Tyler joined his group, leaving Corey standing alone, the last to be chosen.

It had happened many times before, but it always hurt. He laughed and made a little joke about himself as he stepped over to the blue team, but no one listened. They treated him as if he didn't exist, and he felt like it hardly mattered that he did. He wouldn't mind so much being poor at baseball if he had some other skill that his classmates valued. But he was just an average student with no outstanding qualities, and he felt humiliated by his several deficiencies, which he considered serious. He was small and skinny, with thick glasses worn over eyes too poor to see the ball coming until it was too late to catch it or hit it. Corey looked up at Brad, the tall muscular boy who was always chosen first, standing a few feet away, laughing and bantering with the admiring friends who always clustered around him. Corey wished he had the size, the skill, and especially the confidence of Brad. *Why shouldn't they choose me last?* he thought. *Why should they notice me?* Corey couldn't think of one thing that gave him any value in the eyes of his peers.

Brad, meanwhile, wrestled with internal demons of his own. He dreaded when PE was over. It meant that he must leave his friends and go home to face his father. His dad wanted Brad in varsity sports, but his grades had never been good enough, so he was consigned to PE. It was report card day, and he didn't have a single grade above a *C* except for his usual *A+* in PE, which his father did not count. His chemistry grade had dropped, and his math grade continued to hover at a *D*. His father would be furious. Brad had never been able to live up to the standard his dad set for him. He felt like he had always tried to do his best—at least at first—but his grades had never been much above average, and his dad insisted that average wasn't good enough for a Murcheson. His father constantly reminded him of his own high performance in college and rode Brad hard to bring up his grades. Otherwise, he wouldn't be accepted in his father's alma mater. Brad laughed and swaggered with his friends, but he feared that one day they would to learn the truth. Sure he could hit a ball and throw a pass, but that was about it. His father had convinced him that he didn't measure up where it counts. Deep down inside he did not feel that he had real worth.

It doesn't matter whether we are Coreys or Brads; we all need to feel that we are acceptable—that we measure up as human beings. To be affirmed as acceptable validates our sense of self-worth. We need to think that our being here has meaning and purpose and that our lives have value. But many of us are plagued with self-doubts. Like Brad, we may have been conditioned to believe that our worth is based on performance. Or like Corey, we may have inflicted the problem on ourselves. Feeling humiliation for our inadequacies, real or perceived, we may have come to see ourselves through the eyes of others, measuring our self-worth by their standards of value. We all have inadequacies. We all have areas where our skills and capacities don't measure up to those of others. We all have a deep desire to know that in spite of these inevitable deficiencies, we are acceptable anyway. We have a built-in basic yearning to be embraced for who we are regardless of what we have done, regardless of our skills, and regardless of our appearance. We desire to know that we have inherent value that is unconditional, not dependent on performance, abilities, or looks. We long to be considered a treasure of great worth simply for who we are and not merely for what we do.

The Isolation of Not Feeling Accepted

Young people are usually loaded with insecurities. In the process of self-discovery, they have a natural tendency to wonder whether they measure up. Most think they do not because, like Corey, they compare themselves with peers who seem to have it all together, and the differences they see lead to self-doubt.

Like Brad, most young people tend to adopt a façade of bravado to cover these insecurities, little suspecting that all other kids have constructed the same kind of façade for the same reasons. Corey would have been greatly surprised to learn that Brad could possibly have feelings of inadequacy. But inside, both boys were asking the same basic question: "With my deficiencies, am I really worth anything?" Brad covered his insecurity with a show of overconfidence based on his skill at sports, which his peers valued. But hidden deeply inside, possibly even from himself, was the question: "When anyone gets to know me intimately, will he or she find me acceptable?" The story of the teen years is a search for acceptance—from parents, from peers, from other adults, from anyone who will know them for who they are and yet accept them and validate their worth.

As I travel about the country, I am continually amazed at how many of the young people I meet have known only conditional acceptance or virtually no acceptance at all.

Mark is convinced that he can never get into college because when he was younger, a teacher constantly told him he was stupid. Worse yet, his parents reinforced his low self-image by calling him lazy and telling him he would never amount to anything. So he makes a joke of it and deliberately acts stupid to get laughs from his friends.

Lori grew up with her friends taunting her unmercifully about her skinny legs. They tagged her with the name "Bird Legs" and teased her with jibes like, "You'd better wear skis in the shower so you won't slip down the drain." Later, as a junior in college, Lori filled out to become beautiful—shapely and well-proportioned—while many of her friends battled weight problems. Yet she could not shed the low self-image that had imprinted itself on her mind. She still saw herself as skinny, often apologizing for her bird legs and avoiding situations where she would have to wear a swimsuit in view of others.

Jeff is at the top of his class academically and a starter on the varsity football squad. He comes across to everyone as self-assured and confident. But he exhausts himself and worries continually to maintain his grades and skills, thinking the moment he fails to excel, others will perceive him as a nobody.

In people like Mark and Lori, a poor sense of self-worth is easy to spot because they openly admit their insecurities and negative opinions about themselves. People like Jeff, however, try to hide their uncertainty about themselves by overachieving or by adopting a brash, aggressive attitude. But deep down inside, the problem is the same. They are all insecure and unsure that they are acceptable because they doubt that they have real value apart from how they look or what they do.

Kids with such insecurities about their self-worth go through the world feeling that they are on the outside looking in. Each feels that his or her own inadequacies are huge and debilitating while others seem to have it all together because their inadequacies, if any, are minimal and insignificant. The result is often a sense of isolation spawned by the feeling of being a misfit, of not belonging in the society of the talented, competent, and good-looking. These feelings vanish or at least greatly diminish when they come to know that they are accepted unconditionally in spite of their looks or talents. When this deep need for unconditional acceptance is not met, however, these feelings can become debilitating and lead to depression and possibly even to thoughts of suicide.

The Viewpoint Gap

In the last quarter of the last century, there was much talk about a generation gap. The term referred to the changes in societal attitudes that occur from one generation to the next, and how the previous generation tended not to comprehend fully the changes in society that formed the mindset of their children. Now with the pervasiveness of media and the almost universal access to personal computers in America, those changes are coming too fast for anyone to assimilate. Many adults don't have a clue to the thinking and philosophy that now shapes the outlook of our young people. As a result, many kids feel disconnected from adults today. And without this vital connection, they lack that tether of security they need to remain grounded as they explore who they are. Adults still need to provide that connection. In the pre-adolescent years, both parties usually feel the connection and enjoy it. Little kids think adults know everything. The way Daddy and Mommy do things is the only way they should be done, and their trusting dependence gives them a solid connecting point with adults. But at the onset of adolescence, everything changes. No longer do kids think Mommy and Daddy know everything; they often seem to wonder if their parents know *anything*. It's not as easy for adults to provide their children a sense of security in the wake of this changing outlook. In the teen years, young people begin to test the tether. They experiment with the limits, veer closer to the edge, and even cross the line into unacceptable behavior. Adults often respond ineffectively because they fail to comprehend the shift in viewpoints that dominates young people today.

The generation gap has worsened. It has become a "viewpoint gap," dividing the very way that adults and adolescents approach reality. For example, Jason wants to get a part-time job so he can buy CDs and a new sound system. His parents tell him a part-time job will eat into his already-sparse study time and hurt his schoolwork. They suggest that he needs to adjust his priorities. He is being too materially minded, putting too much emphasis on entertainment and pleasure rather than bettering himself for a responsible future. They admonish him to set his mind on "treasures in heaven" rather than storing up "treasures on earth." They have no intent of rejecting Jason or putting him down as a person. They love him dearly, and they are convinced that they are helping him by denying his desire for a part-time job.

After several unhappy confrontations on the subject, Jason now keeps more to himself and becomes distant and moody. His parents think he is merely being immature and hardheaded at the moment. They are convinced that if they just hold their course, he will in time come to his senses and realize they are doing what is best for him.

But from Jason's point of view the problem looks altogether different. He thinks his parents are putting him down as a person. Music is so important to Jason and his peers that when his parents reject his desire to improve his sound system, he thinks they are rejecting him personally. He can't separate his wants and felt needs from who he is. He feels that they don't accept him unconditionally but only on the basis of his conformity to their values.

Jason is a victim of the postmodern outlook with its new definition of tolerance. Influenced by the belief that each person creates his or her own truth and each truth is to be considered right for that individual, young people today tend to think it is their duty to tolerate all versions of truth and accept each of them as equally valid. With this philosophy dominating their thinking, they can't separate who they are from what they believe. Reject their beliefs and they think you reject them.

The viewpoint gap between Jason and his parents is easy to see. To the previous generation, tolerance meant allowing freedom to believe differently without endorsing the belief—separating the person from his or her ideas or activity. That is how Jason's parents approached him. They rejected their son's priorities but not their son. Jason, on the other hand, feels that his individuality is not being considered. From his viewpoint, his parents will not accept him for who he is. To make him acceptable, they are trying to change him into a copy of themselves and intolerantly forcing their religious views on him. He doesn't see how their Christianity meets his personal needs. To him their religion looks like a list of repressive oughts and ought-nots—hoops everyone must jump through to placate a disapproving God. He thinks his parents are intolerant and that they are forcing him to conform to a template—pushing him into a one-size-fits-all box.

The Need for Unconditional Acceptance

Jason's story illustrates how much of the insecurity that young people feel comes from their impression that adults don't accept them unconditionally. This feeling of innate unacceptability tends to spill over into all areas of their lives. They feel that they are not accepted unconditionally anywhere—that they must earn acceptance by performing according to a standard. To meet such expectations, young people will usually do one of two things: (1) They will try to prove their worthiness by performing. They think that only if they make the team, only if their report card shows *A's* and *B's*, only if they have the right friends, or only if they attend Sunday school will they be acceptable. They will try their best to jump through all the hoops and feel a constant sense of insecurity due to fear of failure, or (2) their failure to meet the standard will discourage them, and they will capitulate to their feelings of rejection, give up trying, and drop out. They will write off winning approval as hopeless. They will tune out the criticism and the harping at home, isolate themselves in their rooms, and lose themselves in their computers and music. They will resist the constant pressure to perform and resign themselves to rejection, building a façade or a hardened shell to insulate themselves from the hurt. Building such a protective device does not mean they will give up their search for unconditional acceptance. That desire is too strong to stifle or ignore. They will seek acceptance among peers like themselves who are also victims of the view-point gap. They will commiserate with such peers and adopt a common view that adults and church are the enemies.

Many kids and adults have unwittingly fallen into the performance trap without even realizing it. Parents, teachers, and youth workers intent on helping their young people grow up to be responsible adults often prod them toward good behavior in ways that unwittingly foster the idea that performance is the path to approval. They don't understand how kids can see such efforts as a devaluation of their innate worth. Since today's kids do not easily separate what they think and do from who they are, adult efforts to change them can engender the feeling that they are innately unacceptable. Adults dealing with young people must learn to focus first on the solid truth that God's love is unconditional and gives every human being innate worth regardless of what he or she thinks or does. Kids like Corey who are often chosen last, or like Lori who feel diminished by a physical deficiency, would not feel worthless if they learned to hold firmly to the truth that God values them beyond human comprehension simply for who they are.

A Healthy Sense of Self-Worth

Many well-meaning Christians doubt that it is biblical to view ourselves as having value or worth. They believe that the concept of self-worth fosters the sin of pride by focusing attention on self rather than on God. Of course, people can become self-centered, and they often do wrap themselves up in self-interest. But far from making us prideful, a proper understanding of our worth and value as God's creation is exactly what keeps us from becoming selfish and self-centered. The psalmist wrote, "What are mortals that you should think of us, mere humans that you should care for us? For you made us only a little lower than God, and you crowned us with glory and honor" (Psalm 8:4–5, NLT). This Scripture tells us that we have value not because of our own efforts, not because of anything we do or don't do, but simply because God crowns us like kings or queens with immense value. Our self-worth is rooted in the value he places on us. That certainly does not give us cause for pride but rather for amazement and humility. What could the creator and master of the universe possibly see in us? We may not understand, but we dare not contradict his estimation of us by pretending a false humility that lowers our worth below the high price he has placed on us and paid for us.

Even if your young person is regarded as a nobody on the ball field, in his or her social group, in the classroom, or even at home, that person is somebody to God. Even if a boy or girl is not perceived as good-looking, talented, or accomplished, his or her infinite worth and value to God is undiminished. A healthy self-worth really comes down to seeing yourself as God sees you.

Students who cultivate a healthy, biblical sense of self-worth can accept themselves as God accepts them because they know even when they are the last chosen or their legs are too skinny that God loves them dearly and delights in them. This acceptance is not based on the way they look or anything they have done, but on the fact that God created them in his image and sent his Son to die for them. Biblical self-worth believes, "I am lovable, and I have reason and purpose for existence. I am far from perfect, but God has forgiven me and redeemed me. Through his power, I can become all he wants me to be." Obviously, young people who develop such a sense of self-worth will feel secure and acceptable. They will believe that they matter infinitely and that God created them for a purpose. With such a healthy view of self, they will not be slaves to the opinions of their peers and the adults in their lives. They will be free to be themselves, and they will be better prepared to interact and connect with parents and other adults. These kids will radiate hope, joy, and trust.

The purpose of this chapter has been simply to show the universal need for unconditional acceptance and the negative self-image which results from falling into the performance trap. In the next two chapters, we will show you how God accepts us unconditionally and how parents and caregivers to youth can model unconditional acceptance to their young people.

CHAPTER 8

How Christ Meets Our Need for Unconditional Acceptance

People had looked down on Zacchaeus his entire life. He was a short man, and no doubt ever since his teen years, he had been taunted for his diminutive size. Feeling insignificant in the eyes of others, he may well have set out to prove his worth, both to himself and to others, by becoming rich. We can imagine him saying, "I'll show them. I will make them accept me. This little man is about to become a big man. I will earn their respect by becoming wealthy. Everyone respects wealth, no matter how it's gained. Doors open for the rich, and the red carpet rolls out everywhere." So this Jewish man became a tax collector for the Romans, the hated conquerors of the Jews who occupied their land. Ambitious to succeed, he quickly learned all the tricks of the trade—how to smell out a lie about hidden money, how to gouge the rich with threats and blackmail, how to get merchants and farmers to pay twice what they owed, and how to pry the last denari from a homeless widow.

It didn't take Zacchaeus long to become one of the best and wealthiest collectors in the land. Just as he had predicted, people no longer treated him as a nobody. But somehow this newfound "respect" didn't satisfy him. Even though everyone bowed and scraped and addressed him with oily compliments, he could see the hate in their eyes, and waves of guilt washed over his conscience. He knew they were not really accepting him as a person but rather were fearing him for what he could do to them and loathing him for conniving with the Roman oppressors. In terms of real acceptance, Zacchaeus was no better off than when he had nothing.

It could well have been this sense of rejection and isolation that drove this little man into the street when he heard that the itinerant rabbi Jesus was coming to Jericho. He had heard stories of what Jesus had done in other cities—healings, exorcisms, feeding huge crowds with almost nothing, and of his clashes with the self-righteous Pharisees. He likely had no idea that Jesus could or would do anything for him, yet that sense of restless need drove him into the gathering hordes walking toward the main road. Luke tells us that "Zacchaeus was a small man, and he couldn't see Jesus because of the crowd. So Zacchaeus ran ahead and climbed a fig tree to see Jesus, who was coming that way. When Jesus came to the tree, he looked up and said, 'Zacchaeus, come down! I must stay at your house today.' Zacchaeus came down and was glad to welcome Jesus into his home" (Luke 19:3–6).

Luke goes on to tell us that the crowds were upset at Jesus for dining with such a person. To eat a meal with a man was to accept him, and Zacchaeus was too notorious a sinner to be acceptable. We know nothing about the dinnertime conversation between Zacchaeus and Jesus that day, but we do know that the contact changed the tax collector's life. Luke tells us that Zacchaeus said to Jesus, "Lord, I'll give half of my property to the poor. I'll pay four times as much as I owe to those I have cheated in any way" (Luke 19:8).

When Christ passed beneath that tree, he knew everything about Zacchaeus—all his sordid past of cheating and extortion. Jesus could easily have looked up and rebuked the man clinging to those branches and demanded that he repent of his evil past to avoid the fires of hell. But instead, he extended to him the cultural sign of total acceptance: "Zacchaeus, let's you and I sit down and eat a meal together." And the result of this friendly invitation was to transform the tax collector into a new man.

Suppose Jesus had chosen to rebuke Zacchaeus for his many sins. Would the result have been the same? Not likely. Jesus understood the man's deep need for acceptance. It was true that Zacchaeus had spent his life trying to meet that need in inappropriate ways, but Jesus chose to accept him in spite of his sin. He showed him that acceptance has nothing to do with what a man does but with who he is. Jesus saw Zacchaeus' deep need for acceptance, and he met that need before he did anything else. Because of Christ's loving acceptance, the man's barriers came down, and he was willing to address the fact of deep sin in his life and repent of it.

Today, after hearing a man address sin in his life and commit to reform, the popular tendency would be to try to make him feel good about himself by downplaying the seriousness of his sin. "Oh, that's all right. You probably didn't mean it. We all sin, and yours is no worse than anyone else's. You need not feel so bad about it. You don't have to make restitution to everyone you have wronged; it's all water under the bridge now." But Jesus said nothing like that. Rather he was quick to endorse Zacchaeus' assessment of his wrongs and his commitment to set things right. He responded, "You and your family have been saved today" (Luke 19:9). When Zacchaeus chose to let go of his sinful ways, then Jesus exulted in his decision, for it meant that Zacchaeus had jettisoned the baggage that would prevent him from living eternally in the presence of the holy God.

Acceptance Versus Tolerance

Jesus' treatment of the tax collector is significant because it shows that he separated Zacchaeus the man from the sins that he had committed. He accepted the man but not the man's behavior. Notice that the crowd watching Jesus and Zacchaeus could not make that distinction. Luke tells us that the crowds were displeased. "He went to be the guest of a sinner," they grumbled (Luke 19:7). In their eyes Zacchaeus' behavior was contemptible; therefore, Zacchaeus was contemptible.

It's the flip side of what we see happening today. The cultural mindset is conditioning us to think that a person's attitudes, values, behavior, and lifestyle define who he or she is. But instead of *rejecting* the person because his activity is unacceptable, the order of the day is to turn the error on its head and insist that we *accept* all of a person's choices and behaviors—regardless of how much they flout absolute morality—along with the person. As in the days of Zacchaeus, today's wisdom still ties a person's value to his or her behavior. It says that to reject a person's choices is to reject the person. Rather than label anyone unacceptable, we are urged to endorse every lifestyle and behavior choice. Rather than hurt people by condemning them because of their bad behavior, we are expected to remove all value judgments that would cause us to label anything wrong so that we can tolerate all behavior. I'm OK; you're OK, no matter what either of us do or think. On the surface, exercising this kind of tolerance seems the loving thing to do. It avoids condemnation and increases acceptance for everyone.

But such an attitude is far from loving. As I wrote in my book, *The New Tolerance* (with Bob Hostetler), the real opposite of love is not hate but indifference.[1] The current emphasis on tolerance of all choices and lifestyles is the indifferent, easy way to deal with people. It is a cop-out. It is selfish and uncaring because it says essentially, "I don't care enough about you to get involved in the hassle of confrontation required to deal with the behavior that is destroying you." If you love a person, you will not accept his drug addiction or homosexuality as a viable lifestyle choice. If you love a person you will not accept her destructive sexual behavior as just "who she is."

Such acceptance in the name of tolerance is really indifference. It is a backhanded rejection of people because it tells them you don't think they have enough innate value to be worth confronting. Acceptance in the current way of thinking says, "If you accept me, you must approve of what I think and do." But love must respond, "No, I must do something harder: I must plead with you to change your behavior or lifestyle because I think you are worth the effort."

This is exactly how Jesus accepted people. He accepted them unconditionally because he saw through their behavior and found beneath it persons of immense worth. Because they were of immense worth, he refused to tolerate behavior that he knew would destroy their lives and cause them to miss out on a relationship with him. The apostle John tells us of the incident in Samaria where Jesus was alone at the town well, waiting for his disciples, when a woman came to draw water. "Please give me a drink," Jesus said. The woman stopped in her tracks, shocked that he would ask. She was doubly shocked because in that society men would not speak to women in public, and Jews held Samaritans in such contempt that they would not talk with them at all. Yet here was a Jew who was accepting her simply as a person, in spite of her race and gender.

The surprised woman responded, "'How can a Jewish man like you ask a Samaritan woman like me for a drink of water?' Jesus replied to her, 'If you only knew what God's gift is and who is asking you for a drink, you would have asked him for a drink. He would have given you living water'" (John 4:9–10). Of course, at first the woman did not understand him. But soon she realized that he was speaking of water metaphorically and that the living water he offered was an eternally satisfying love in a permanent relationship such as she had never known. As she began to feel a deep thirst for what Jesus offered, he told her to go get her husband.

"The woman replied, 'I don't have a husband.' Jesus told her, 'You're right when you say that you don't have a husband. You've had five husbands, and the man you have now isn't your husband. You've told the truth'" (John 4:17–18).

Jesus knew that this woman was craving something more than just water from the well. She had deeper needs for the kind of love and acceptance that she was sorely missing. Rejection was the story of her life. Five husbands had left her, and even now she clung to a man who would not commit to her. No doubt the reason she came to the well at midday was to avoid facing the rejection of all the other women who drew their water first thing in the morning. She was not acceptable in their company because she had chosen a lifestyle that shut her out from her own people. Jesus saw not only her value; he also saw her need to be accepted.

Before he did anything else, he accepted her unconditionally. He treated her simply as a person of worth without investigation or reprimand. He knew her sin, but he saw past it to the woman within whom he loved dearly. He affirmed her worth by accepting her for who she was, where she was, in spite of her lifestyle, and offering her the promise of a relationship so satisfying she would never again need to thirst for the love she so desperately craved.

But Jesus did not stop there. He led this Samaritan woman to confront the sin in her life that stood between her and joy. He knew that she was clinging to something that would separate her from the fulfilling love for which she thirsted. It would not have been loving for him to affirm her lifestyle as her own legitimate choice and leave her in the descending spiral that would end in a fatal crash. She was immensely valuable to him, and he loved her, so he did all he could to separate her from the sin that would have destroyed her forever.

But Are We Really Acceptable?

We all long for the same kind of acceptance that Zacchaeus and the Samaritan woman craved. We would not crave acceptance so much if we felt a confident assurance that we are acceptable. We doubt our acceptability because we are loaded with guilt feelings about things we have done. And we doubt it with good reason. The truth is, we are not very acceptable. Those guilt feelings are not merely psychosomatic; they are real. We feel guilty because we are guilty. We are contaminated with sin. We have done terrible, selfish things that are abhorrent to God and appalling even to ourselves.

The Pharisees of Jesus' day believed that the presence of sin in one's life meant automatic rejection. They believed that our choices determined our value. Those who made good choices had high value, and those who made selfish, sinful choices had no value. The truth is, if it were not for one, crucially important fact, these Pharisees would be absolutely correct. Our sin would contaminate us and make us unacceptable to God. But that one fact makes all the difference.

That one fact, of course, is the coming of Christ. Christ came to earth to make it possible to separate the person from his or her sin. Had it not been for him, our sin would have been so inextricably bound up with who we are that we would have been forever unacceptable to God. But God's incredible love for us moved him to find a way to make us acceptable again. The utter holiness of his nature meant he had to deal with our sin before he could find us acceptable. He had to separate the sin from the person so the sin could be destroyed and the person saved. The only way it could be done was to pay the ultimate price himself. So God came down and died, taking the guilt of sin on himself so that we could be free from it. Because he gave us a way of removing sin, he is now able to look beneath the sin we carry and see us for the treasure that he created us to be. Because of his sacrifice, he can see us separately from our sin. He can move toward us in acceptance and show us our need to get rid of sin, as he did for Zacchaeus and the Samaritan woman.

On the surface, the need to remove sin before our relationship with God can be restored may make it seem that God does not really accept us unconditionally. The sin must be removed; isn't that a condition? But Christ's coming shows how much he loved us and longed for us even before the removal of our sin had been accomplished. The incarnation gives us proof that God accepts us unconditionally in the fact that he came after us while we were yet sinners. As the apostle Paul says it, "Christ died for us while we were still sinners. This demonstrates God's love for us" (Romans 5:8). With his foreknowledge, God knew you before you were born. He loved you and wanted you. He could not stand the thought of losing you to the fatal disease of sin. Even knowing that you would be born into a world of sin and that you would accumulate a contaminating load of guilt, he looked at the innate value that he gave you in creation and found you worth dying for.

He found you innately acceptable, though in his innate holiness he could not accept your sin. He came to separate you from your sin so that he could enjoy a relationship with you forever.

The sacrifice of Christ on the cross enables him to say to each of us, "I still see in you the immense value that I placed in you when you were created. I love you dearly, and I want you for my own. I love you in spite of your sin. I accept you for who you are, but before you can be mine, we must do something about that sin. I have given you a way to get rid of it. You can turn it over to me, and I will take it into the grave and bury it forever. As much as I long to do this for you, I will not force you into it. I will let you choose. But know this, if you choose sin over me, it will break my heart because I love you so much that I don't want to lose you forever."

God Accepts You Unconditionally

The fact that God accepts us unconditionally is hard for most of us to assimilate. We have a natural human tendency to think that what we do determines who we are. It's no wonder the new tolerance has come to dominate an increasingly godless society. The guilt people feel is unbearable when they do not understand what God has done to remove it. When you take God out of the equation, the only way to deal with inevitably sinful behavior is to pretend that sin is not real and treat everyone as if nothing they do or believe is really evil.

The idea that sin ruins our innate value is pervasive among many Christians as well, even though they know that Christ died to remove our guilt. Some think that God can forgive lesser sins, or he can forgive people who merely slip a little now and then. But many believe they have sinned so grievously that they have fallen beyond his acceptance.

Richard was a prominent minister in the town. He constantly drove his daughter Eva to walk a straight line. She had to be a model of Christian perfection in purity and behavior. Any time she slipped or even gave the appearance of slipping, he always punished her severely with groundings, keeping her from social events and giving her stern lectures on uprightness. In her senior year, Eva killed herself by starting her car and sitting in it with the garage closed. Richard was devastated, but he understood when they found Eva's note. She had discovered that she was pregnant, and she could not stand facing her father with the fact. Richard, pastor though he was, blamed himself and could not believe that God would forgive him. He resigned his ministry and quit the church, convinced that he was doomed to hell for killing his daughter. He told people, "After what I've done, God cannot possibly forgive me or love me any more."

The world is full of people like Richard who think they have fallen beyond God's reach. The effects of their sin are so irrevocable and devastating that they cannot forgive themselves, and thus, they believe that God cannot forgive them. Others who have sinned grievously think they must take steps to re-qualify themselves before they can again become acceptable to God. They feel that they must turn from some vice, start regular church attendance, memorize Bible verses, or give more money to the church, and then God can accept them.

Both of these ideas are wrong. As the subtitle of one of Max Lucado's books says, *You Cannot Fall Beyond God's Love*. His love is not earned; one does not have to qualify for it; it is simply there.

God's love is a family thing. You love and accept your daughter simply because she is yours. It doesn't matter whether she is beautiful or plain, intelligent or slow, a model of behavior or a continuing source of frustration. You simply love her. Your son may keep you awake at nights worrying about his lifestyle or beliefs, but you still love him. And it won't matter what he does in the future. Whether he ends up president of the United States or a convict in the penitentiary, you will continue to love him. You loved your child before he or she was even born. You talked to him while he was still in the womb. You planned her nursery, put aside money for his education, and spent hours lovingly choosing just the right name for her. You didn't wait for him to be born to see whether he would be acceptable. You accepted her because she belonged to you.

God feels the same way about his children. It doesn't matter how you turn out—success or failure, beautiful or plain—he loves you. Even though we were born sinners, even though we had become enemies of God, he accepted us as being of great value and loved us dearly.

Obviously, that love was not based on anything we did because it was there before we were born. We did not earn it. Nothing in our performance or behavior made us deserve it. God loved us in spite of the deadly infection of sin that doomed us to death. "God is rich in mercy because of his great love for us. We were dead because of our failures, but he made us alive together with Christ. (It is God's kindness that saved you)" (Ephesians 2:4–5).

God came to earth to offer his grace when we were too helpless even to know our problem or ask for help. No matter who we are, no matter what we've done, no matter how heavy our sin, he starts there. We don't have to qualify for his redeeming love. He accepts us where we are, dirt and all, and loves us in spite of it.

The image of God that many Christians carry around is that of a stern judge watching every move and ready to zap anyone who commits a sin. That image fosters the performance syndrome that many Christians still have. They feel they must earn God's acceptance by doing good works and being good church members. That concept of a condemning God is as far from the truth as east is from west. God does not want you condemned; that's why his Son died for you. He has been called "the hound of heaven" because of his relentless pursuit of sinners. If you miss out on his loving acceptance, it is simply because you choose to reject it.

Let's look again at the incident in Jesus' life when the scribes and Pharisees brought to him the woman taken in adultery. The self-righteous mob found her unacceptable because of her immoral behavior, and they were eager to condemn her. When they insisted on stoning her to death, Jesus said, "'The person who is sinless should be the first to throw a stone at her.' Then he bent down again and continued writing on the ground. One by one, beginning with the older men, the scribes and Pharisees left. Jesus was left alone with the woman. Then Jesus straightened up and asked her, 'Where did they go? Has anyone condemned you?' The woman answered, 'No one, sir.' Jesus said, 'I don't condemn you either. Go! From now on don't sin'" (John 8:7,10–11). Jesus, the only person there with a right to condemn the woman, saw great value in her and forgave her. But he did not overlook her sin. He knew her immoral behavior would destroy her, and he loved her too much to dismiss it as inconsequential. As he sent her on her way, he commanded her to "sin no more." But remember that the first thing he did was to accept her as a valuable person worth saving.

CHAPTER 9

Modeling Unconditional Acceptance

EMS sirens blared as the ambulance whipped around the corner and sped to the hospital. Nurses and doctors made way as attendants wheeled the injured girl down the hallway and into the emergency room where they stopped beneath clusters of monitors, tubes, and IV stands. The young woman on the gurney moaned with the pain of the bruises, the bleeding lacerations on her head, and her broken ribs and arm. As the ER attendants hurried to staunch her wounds and hook her to monitors, the doctor slowly sauntered in, frowning at the chart in his hand.

"Please, help me!" the hurting girl moaned.

"Quiet!" snapped the doctor. "Can't you see I'm reading your accident report?" After a long moment he looked up and took a step toward the gurney, but he stopped short at the splashes of blood on the floor. "Just look at the mess you're making in here! And all over our clean sheets, too!"

"I'm sorry," said the injured girl. "But please, help me. I'm in such pain."

"You should have thought of that before you had your accident," retorted the doctor, still standing away from the bed. "According to this report, it was all your fault. You ran a stop sign and broadsided another car. You should have thought then of the pain your action would cause. You should have thought of the injuries you caused to the people in the other car. But no, you didn't think at all, did you? You just drove as you pleased, and now you come in here, messing up the place, and expect me to fix everything back like it was. That's just like young people these days. You ignore the rules, then when things go wrong, you run to us to put things right again. Well, young lady, I'm going to teach you a lesson. I'm going to let you hurt and bleed for a while, and maybe next time you'll think twice before you act so recklessly." With that the doctor turned on his heel and walked out the door.

Of course, no doctor would ever treat an emergency patient— or any patient—the way this physician treated the injured girl. A good doctor drops everything and provides the needed comfort and healing, regardless of what caused the patient's illness or injuries. Any physician will accept the patient where she is and do whatever is necessary to bring her to health. Yet many religious people have treated (and still treat) hurting people who bring the hurt on themselves with this kind of disdain. When the Pharisees of Jesus' day criticized him for socializing with notorious sinners, he replied, "Healthy people don't need a doctor; those who are sick do." And to be sure they got the point, he went on to say, "I've come to call sinners, not those who don't think they have any flaws" (Matthew 9:12–13).

Jesus did not accept people on the basis of their good performance; he accepted them in spite of it. He accepted people because he loved them as persons even when their performance was abysmal as we have shown in the cases of Zacchaeus and the woman at the well. Christ's love drove him to accept them, and their need drew him to minister to them. Our privilege as Christians is to show this same kind of unconditional acceptance to those we encounter in our own lives. What does this unconditional acceptance look like today? The following story gives us a clue.

The lunch bell rang, and the sudden din of scraping chairs, closing books, and simultaneous chatter filled the room in Mrs. Keeler's sophomore speech class. "One more thing before you leave," she shouted over the noise. "I need to know how many of you will try out for the debate team on Monday." Five of her best students raised their hands. Mrs. Keeler noticed that Lisa, sitting quietly on the back row, looked up, her eyes momentarily bright, then sadly looked down again without raising her hand.

As the kids streamed out the door and headed for the lunchroom, Lisa held back, as usual. The girl always waited until the others were occupied with their friends and on their way out before she gathered her things to leave. She had no friends—at least, not any more. The other girls seldom spoke to her now—not even her former friends in the church youth group. And Mrs. Keeler knew why. Just three weeks ago, Lisa had returned from an extended stay with an aunt in New England "to deal with a health problem" as her parents had explained. But everyone knew the real reason: Lisa had become pregnant and had been sent away to have the baby.

After Mrs. Keeler filled her lunch tray, she looked across the lunchroom and saw Lisa sitting alone at a corner table. Instead of taking her meal to the teachers' lounge as she usually did, she made her way to Lisa's table. "Lisa, may I sit here?" she asked.

"Sure, I guess so," said the girl without looking up.

After a few attempts at conversation about clothes, movies, and music, Mrs. Keeler said, "Lisa, I would really like for you to try out for the debating team."

Lisa glanced up, her eyes momentarily brightening, but the gleam quickly faded. "I—I couldn't. The other team members, they—they wouldn't like—"

"Lisa, you are an excellent thinker," Mrs. Keeler interrupted. "Your papers show that you zero right in to the heart of a subject and organize your thoughts logically. You would really be an asset to the team. Will you please try out?"

"But, you know what I've done," replied Lisa, her voice quivering. "The school wouldn't want someone like me representing them at contests."

"Of course we want you!" said Mrs. Keeler.

"But the others on the team . . ."

"Lisa, let me tell you something about me that you don't know. When I was about your age, I too became pregnant. But I did something even worse. I slipped away and had an abortion. When my mother found out, she told me I was not only a fornicator but also a murderer. Although I continued to live in her house, she was very cold to me. From that time on, she never again hugged me or said anything kind. Her rejection convinced me that God could no longer accept me either. For years, I felt a terrible guilt. Then in college, I met Bert, a seminary student who showed me how Christ accepted people in spite of what they've done. He insisted that Christ also accepted me and loved me. But for a long time, I simply would not believe it could be true."

"What changed your mind?" asked Lisa, now listening with real interest.

"It was when Bert Keeler proposed," replied Mrs. Keeler, smiling as moisture brimmed in her happy eyes. "At that moment it hit me. Bert's full acceptance in spite of my past drove home the truth that God could do the same thing. Bert was a living demonstration of God's unconditional acceptance of me."

Suddenly Lisa flashed the most radiant smile that her teacher had ever seen on her face. "Just as you are a living demonstration of his unconditional acceptance of me," she said. "Yes, Mrs. Keeler, I think I will try out for the debating team!"

Accepting Others In Spite of What They Have Done

Lisa's friends and Mrs. Keeler's mother fell into a trap that snares many of us who deal with young people. We want so much for our kids to grow up productive and responsible that we unwittingly slip into the performance trap. Naturally, we want the best for our kids, and therefore, we also want the best *from* them— good grades, moral behavior, right choices, Christian friends, a sense of responsibility, and good habits. Such behavior attributes are landmarks on the road to a good life, and it is our responsibility to help our young people along the way. Acting on these good intentions, parents and youth workers sometimes unwittingly find themselves showing acceptance when kids follow the rules and stay out of trouble but turning cool and critical and seemingly withholding acceptance when they misbehave or fail. Like our fictitious emergency room doctor, adults sometimes use acceptance as a disciplinary tool, granting it for good behavior and withdrawing it for bad.

God's acceptance of us is based not on performance but on who each of us is—a unique human being created in his own image with infinite value, dignity, purpose, and worth. C. S. Lewis tells us that in all our interactions with others we should maintain an acute awareness of this immense God-instilled value that resides in every human. He calls us to recognize that "the dullest and most uninteresting person you can talk to may one day be a creature which, if you saw it now, you would be strongly tempted to worship . . . There are no *ordinary* people. You have never talked to a mere mortal. Nations, cultures, arts, civilizations—these are mortal, and their life to ours is as the life of a gnat."[1] God created us for such splendor that it staggers the imagination to think how glorious we will be when he restores us to his original intent.

Of course, in our day-to-day dealings with each other, it's not always easy to see the jewel that each of us is because of all the mud that obscures it. But beneath that pimply face, the spiked hair, the baggy jeans, the ring in the eyebrow, the dirty room, and the hours on the phone exists a treasure that is worth more to God than heaven itself. All dealings with our young people must be carried out on the basis of our recognition of that worth. The more firmly we grasp their immense inherent value, the more intimately we can bond with them. We must first show that we accept our kids where they are and for what they are—a masterpiece of God's creation—apart from their behavior and then deal as necessary with the behavior. Treating them as persons of value gives them security in their relationships. If they don't feel secure in their relationships with us, our efforts to alter their behavior or lead them to conviction about Christ have only a limited chance of success.

This kind of treatment of our young people is easier if we hold firmly to the fact that it is exactly how God treats us. He understands our weaknesses, our failures, and our sins, yet he loves us dearly and accepts us in spite of it all. We know this to be true because, as we pointed out in the previous chapter, he died for us while *we were yet sinners*. We didn't earn this acceptance; he didn't wait for us to deserve it; it was not based on our good performance or anything we achieved. It was there from the start, even before we were born. It's a family thing. He loves and accepts us because we belong to him, just as we love and accept the baby still in the womb. We demonstrate this unconditional acceptance by accepting our kids in the same way—in spite of their performance, simply because they are created by God who endowed them with immense value.

Acceptance and Discipline

"But," one may object, "we adults must discipline and guide our young people. It's our duty. These are just kids, and kids make mistakes. They need discipline and correction to help them make right choices. We've got to come down on them when they need discipline, don't we?"

Of course we must discipline, and that sometimes means being firm and restrictive. But often well-meaning parents misunderstand what we explained in chapter seven—that young people today, immersed in the postmodern outlook of their generation, tend to feel that when we reject their choices, we reject them personally. That means we must take great care that acceptance precedes discipline.

As we have already explained, the key is to separate the person from the behavior. But this means more than simply "hating the sin but loving the sinner." We must go one step further. We must deal with the pain that accompanies disobedience and failure. We cannot simply love our young people yet hate what they do while we let them keep on doing it. That is not acceptance; it is indifference. We cannot comply with the cultural call that says, "If you love me, you will endorse all my choices and behavior." If we love them, we must protect their health, happiness, and spiritual growth. It's not loving to let the child play in the street, to give out condoms, or to turn our eyes away from marijuana in order to avoid giving the child feelings of rejection. Real love grieves over the consequences of wrong behavior and seeks to prevent and correct it.

Yes, we must guide and discipline our kids, and that means learning the key to loving confrontation. I (Tom) remember in my own childhood that when my father was about to administer severe discipline he would say, "Now son, this is going to hurt me more than it is you." *Yeah, sure!* I thought. I didn't believe it for a moment. I was often tempted to say, *Well, Dad, then why don't we just forget the whole thing and spare both of us the pain.* But when I had three daughters of my own, I understood exactly what Dad was saying. Discipline is painful, both to the adult and the child. And it should be. The fact that a father or mother feels the pain of his or her child shows a healthy sense of compassion—that the parent is successfully seeing the young person as a human being with feelings and value. For this reason, it is not likely that adults will be successful in demonstrating love while administrating discipline unless they do feel the pain of it themselves.

When we deal with children who make wrong choices or experience failures, our underlying attitude should be, "I want to help you work through this." When your daughter brings home a bad report card, you might say something like, "Karen, I know this *D* in chemistry must bother you. As you know, we have never required that you make straight *A*'s, but your grade has never dipped this low, and I am naturally concerned for you. Are you having trouble understanding the subject? If so, I'll be glad to help you with your homework until you get back on your feet. Is anything else bothering you or distracting you from your work?" If you know Karen is capable of doing better, and her grade is slipping because she spends two hours every night on the phone with her friends, you will likely have to help her rearrange her priorities and enforce them. But if you show that your first concern is for her, the medicine will go down much easier.

Sometimes you face a problem that you must deal with immediately, and you can't slide into it so gracefully.

"Bye, Mom," called sixteen-year-old Ginny as she rushed down the stairs and headed for the door. Her mother glanced up to see that Ginny was wearing a very low-slung, hip-hugging, leather micro-mini skirt and a tight halter top showing her navel and six inches of bare midriff.

"Ginny, where did you get those clothes?" the mother called.

"I borrowed them from Megan. See ya, Mom, I've got to hurry. Kristin is waiting for me." Ginny put her hand on the knob to open the door.

"No, Ginny, I can't let you go out dressed like that."

"But Mom, all the girls dress this way. In fact, compared to most of them, I look like a nun."

"I know how you feel, Ginny. It's really hard when you have to cut against the grain. But you are much too valuable to treat yourself so cheaply. You have a wonderful body, and there's a wonderful you living inside it. I love you too much to let you regard yourself as less than you are worth. You need to protect the treasure that you are as a rare jewel until you can gift wrap it for some special young man to unwrap on your wedding night."

"OK, Mom," Ginny sighed. "I'll go change." She gave her mother a wry grin as she ran back up the stairway.

It was Friday night, and Kerry and Cheryl were planning to drive across town to visit a friend in the hospital. They were leaving their sixteen-year-old son Kent to babysit his seven-year-old brother, Austin. After Austin was put to bed, Kent's friend Denny was coming over to watch a movie. Kerry happened to notice the movie Kent had rented laying on the DVD player. It was a recent R-rated hit containing nudity, heavy sexual themes, and explicit dialogue. Kerry called Kent into the den and said, "Son, I love you too much to let you watch this movie. What you see and take into your mind becomes a part of you and affects your outlook and the way you think. I don't want to see that fine mind of yours contaminated and inflamed by the images and ideas this movie will put into it." He drew a five-dollar bill from his wallet. "Here, you have just enough time before we leave to take this movie back and get something more suited to who you want to become. Later, you and I need to have a little talk about choosing your movies."

Kerry showed acceptance of his son and at the same time corrected him by doing three positive things: he based his reason for forbidding Kent to watch the movie on the boy's high value, he gave his son the means to correct the problem, and he gave him the freedom to make a new decision, along with a solid basis for making it.

Acceptance and Security

We must be sensitive not only in our discipline, but also to the natural vulnerability of young people. Be aware of all those insecurities and uncertainties that accompany discovering who they are as they make the transition from childhood to adulthood. Like Corey who was always chosen last and Lori who was teased for her skinny legs, they often face rejection and ridicule from their peers. Even young people with outstanding abilities often feel rejection when they fail to meet the higher expectations created by their talents. They desperately need affirmation of their innate worth in the form of adult acceptance.

Carlos, the starting wide receiver on the high school football team, dropped the last-second touchdown pass that hit him right in the hands as he stepped into the end zone. The pass would have won the game and given his team the district crown. But instead they lost both the game and district. The boy felt lower than a throw rug. He had let his team down, as well as the school and the community.

After the game the coach caught up with the dejected boy as he walked toward his car, "Carlos, I know how much dropping that pass must have hurt you, and I hurt with you. I know the pain you must feel because I've made mistakes that caused me to feel the same way. I know you would give anything for a chance to replay that down. I just want you to know that this makes no difference in the way I feel about you. You have been a good team player, and you have always given your all. I have always been proud of you, and I still am. You are still the highly-valued member of this ball club that you have always been. I look forward to having you back on my team next year."

The coach could have tried to make light of Carlos' feelings by saying, "Don't feel so bad, Carlos. Everyone makes mistakes. You've got to swallow this and go on as if it never happened." Instead, he understood the depth of the boy's dejection and affirmed his innate value. He accepted the boy in spite of his failure.

To make young people's needs for discipline and affirmation easier to handle, adults can look for opportunities to show unconditional acceptance "in advance," not driven by any impending crisis, failure, or emergency, thus paving the road for smooth riding when such crises do occur.

I have an excellent relationship with my daughter Kelly. I'm convinced that our closeness is due largely to my efforts to convey acceptance of her regardless of what she does. When she was thirteen, a news story revealing that a well-known Christian leader had been having an adulterous affair shocked her deeply. She wanted to know what I thought about it. I had heard all the condemnation of the leader by other prominent pastors, and I knew that their response was communicating the message, "We will love and accept you as long as you stay pure, but if you get involved in sexual sin, we will condemn you." Kids like Kelly would interpret this message in their own terms: "We will love and accept you if you don't get on drugs, if you don't drink, if you don't get pregnant, if you don't listen to bad music, if you don't dye your hair green, etc."

So after a moment of serious thought, I said, "Kelly, what this man did was wrong. It was sin." I took the time to explain to her why it was wrong, and then I went on. "But you need to realize that God loves him as much as he loves you or me. Christ died for him as much as for any of us. Just as God can forgive you or me, he can forgive this man for what he has done." Then after a little more thought, I went a step further. I took a deep breath, looked her in the face, and said, "Kelly, let's look at it this way. If you got pregnant, can you imagine what your dad would go through because of my message on sexual purity? Half the people here in our own church would turn on me, and my message would lose its impact. Stores would quit selling my material on the subject, and I would no longer be asked to speak on it anywhere."

Kelly looked up at me and said, "I know that, Dad."

"But you need to know one thing more," I continued. "If you ever did get pregnant, I wouldn't care what all those people said. I would never turn my back on you. I would put my arms around you, and we would see it through together."

At that moment, tears welled up in Kelly's eyes; she dropped her books on the pavement and threw her arms around me saying, "I know you would, Daddy!"

Some people may think that in telling Kelly what I did, I took too big a risk. They may see it as almost like granting her a license to sin. She might not be as vigilant against temptation because she knew she could fall back on my love. But I think the opposite is true. Mutual love and trust create a bond so strong it overcomes the risk. A daughter will not want to disappoint a parent who places so much value on her. This kind of acceptance leads to secure relationships. We might be surprised at how much of our young people's good behavior comes simply from not wanting to disappoint loving and accepting parents, teachers, or youth leaders. The more we love, the more we want to please, and when the desire to please is based on love, it is not an attempt to earn acceptance; it is a response in kind to the demonstration of love that unconditional acceptance gives.

"But," some may object, "shouldn't good behavior be based on a desire to please God rather than humans?" Precisely! The major theme of this book is to show how we can introduce God to others in our own behavior toward them. When they respond to us with a loving bond, they are actually responding to God as we demonstrate him to them. They get a taste of what God is like when they see him in us, and from there we can lead them to look above us and see the real source of the love and unconditional acceptance that flows through our behavior like a life-giving river.

Accepting Others for Who They Are

Using behavior as a condition for acceptance is one way that we adults can fail our young people. Another is not to recognize the uniqueness of each of them. Treating Jeremy and Jason or Jennifer and Juanita as if they should be pretty much alike diminishes the value of each because they will think we are "herding" them or forcing them to fit the template instead of valuing their unique individuality. Most parents and people who work with young people learn quickly that what works for one kid will not necessarily work for the next. Keith picks up on the barest suggestions and responds immediately, whereas it takes a two-by-four to get Martin's attention. This fundamental fact points to the obvious need to know the kids you deal with individually and accept them for who they are with all their unique traits. A one-size-fits-all approach will not work.

We're all familiar with the famous admonition in Proverbs, which states "Train up a child in the way he should go, and even when he is old he will not turn away from it" (Proverbs 22:6). This passage is often misunderstood to mean that if we saturate our kids with church, Bible, fellowship, and religious teaching, they will grow up Christian and never depart from the faith. Though that may not be such a bad thing to do, it is not the true meaning of the verse. The phrase, "the way he [or she] should go" refers not to a religious path, but to the child's own way—his or her natural leaning or bent. The key word in the phrase is translated "bend" in two of the psalms and refers to the bending of an archer's bow. In biblical days, archers made their own bows to fit their own strength and unique characteristics. A person could shoot an arrow well only with his own personal bow.

A note on Proverbs 22:6 in the *Ryrie Study Bible* explains that "the way he should go" means according to "the child's habits and interests. The instruction must take into account his individuality and inclinations, his personality, the unique way God created him, and must be in keeping with his physical and mental development."[2] We've all known of fathers with successful careers who pushed their sons to follow in their footsteps, even when the son had a natural bent in another direction. My (Tom's) father was a highly respected preacher. It was clear from an early age that my inclination was toward art, and when I expressed during my high school years the desire to become an illustrator, he didn't try to dissuade me and never urged me to consider the ministry. Instead, he did all he could to help and encourage me toward my goal. He accepted me for who I was. He understood my individuality and did not try to force me into his template. He trained me in the way I should go.

The apostle Paul makes a big thing of our individual uniqueness in 1 Corinthians 12. He explains that as members of the church we are the body of Christ, each with talents and abilities that differ from one another in complementary ways, just as the particular limbs and organs of our physical bodies differ from each other. No two of us are alike, and each is necessary. You are the best you there will ever be. And trying to make you into a copy of me would be a travesty both to you and the world. You would not be happy as an imitation of me, and the world certainly does not need another me!

One reason many young people today shy away from Christianity is their sense that it means the loss of individuality. They think Christians all morph into look-alike widgets stamped out of a production mold that represses full expression of our personhood and dulls our enjoyment of life. They think that becoming a Christian means giving up freedom to be yourself and conforming to a set of rules that dries up spontaneity and stifles individuality and creativity. The opposite is true. In coming to Christ, we liberate our innate personality to be fulfilled to its maximum potential. In him we are free to discover our uniqueness and express it fully. God created each of us different from all others because in our finiteness no one of us can fully reflect his infinite glory. Each of us is designed to reflect one facet of Christ in particular. You can show your mate, your family, your neighbor, your coworkers, a waiter, sales clerk, or mechanic something about God that no one else can. Your role as a member of his body is to reveal that particular facet of God to the rest of creation.

Each of us is like one of the mirrors attached to a mirror ball such as those that hang in skating rinks. We all receive light from a single source, but each of us is angled differently, enabling us to take a beam from that light and reflect it in a direction different from all the others, so that the one primary light source is directed in smaller beams all over the room. Each of us reflects God in a different way. For the image of God to be reflected everywhere depends on each of us doing his or her part. Our connection with him makes us truly individual, for only you can show his light in your particular direction.

The search for meaning that is common to every human— our attempt to "find ourselves"—is really an attempt to find that facet of God that he created us to know and to reflect to others. Each of us is designed to perform a function that no other human on earth can perform, and when we find that function that God has reserved especially for us, we express a special uniqueness that is impossible without him. It takes all Christians acting in concert to give the world a full picture of his character.

God doesn't want to squash our innate characteristics; he wants to develop them, to draw them out and perfect them to their fullest potential. As we will discuss in a later chapter, his goal is not to make us perform, conform, or reform; he wants to *transform* each of us into a clear reflection of his brilliance. He wants to take our latent potential and flip the "on" switch, bringing our unique individuality into full play.

We adults can help our young people toward this goal by accepting them for exactly who they are individually. We can affirm their heart, their creativity, enthusiasm, diligence, persistence, and patience. We can get to know their heart so that we perceive the nature and direction of their deepest desires and bend those desires toward their intended fulfillment in God.

PART II

SECTION 3

God Loves Us Sacrificially

Chapter 10

Our Need for
Sacrificial Love

The O. Henry story "The Gift of the Magi," tells of Jim and Della Young, a poverty-stricken married couple in their early twenties. They have only two material possessions that they value highly. Jim owns a fine gold watch, an heirloom from his grandfather. Lacking money to buy a chain, he keeps the watch on a worn leather strap. Della takes pride in her lustrous cascades of remarkably beautiful hair, which falls almost to her knees. She has yearned to decorate this crowning glory of hers with a set of jeweled, tortoise shell combs she once saw in a shop, but she has no hope of ever owning them because of their high price.

Christmas Eve arrives, and Della has only $1.87, hardly enough to buy Jim a proper gift. In her desperation, she hits on an idea. She sells her hair to a wigmaker for enough money to buy a fine platinum chain for Jim's watch. When Jim comes home from work that night, he stares in shock at his wife's shorn head. She thinks he is angry because he loved her beautiful hair, and she explains that she sold it to buy him a gift. But he is not angry. He takes her in his arms and gives her a package that explains the reason for his shock. He has bought the jeweled tortoise shell combs for her. Eagerly, Della shows him the chain she bought for his watch. "Isn't it a dandy, Jim? I hunted all over town to find it. You'll have to look at the time a hundred times a day now. Give me your watch. I want to see how it looks on it."

Instead of reaching for his watch, Jim smiled. "Dell," said he, "let's put our Christmas presents away and keep 'em a while. They're too nice to use just at present. I sold the watch to get the money to buy your combs."

Could either of these young people help but know that they were deeply loved? Della would never have asked or wanted Jim to sacrifice his most prized possession for her, nor would Jim have asked it of Della. But the sacrificial gifts showed beyond all doubt that each cherished and loved the other more than anything else in their lives. Every one of us has a deep yearning to experience this kind of committed love.

Already in this book, we have explored two other deep needs—our needs for understanding and acceptance. But if you noticed, when we addressed these needs, we often coupled them with the word *love*—"understanding and love," "acceptance and love." Love is the driving force and underlying principle beneath all other needs and all relationships.

The Search for Love

In spite of its high meaning and value, we throw the word *love* around pretty carelessly. We use it in so many ways that it's often hard to be sure just what we mean by it. Women will say things such as, "I just love your new dress" or "I would love to take a cruise to the Bahamas this summer." Men will say "I love my wife" as well as "I love my Ford truck," and though the parallel construction of these phrases should indicate that they mean the same thing, they certainly don't. In trying to make the word mean everything from our taste in movies or chocolates to our sacrificial commitment to a cherished mate, we sometimes throw ourselves into confusion about just what love really means.

Although we incorrectly use the word to describe our taste for inanimate things such as food and music, even when we use it properly it has various meanings. In his book, *The Four Loves*, C. S. Lewis categorizes love into four basic types: friendship, affection, erotic love, and sacrificial love.[1] But many people do not make a clear distinction among these loves, and the resulting problems can be more than merely semantic. We often chase after one kind of love when our deepest need can be satisfied only by another kind.

Perhaps the biggest problem comes from the persistent tendency of today's culture to present love primarily in terms of erotic attraction. Movies, books, magazines, and television all push the idea that the physical connection between a man and a woman is the basis for living happily ever after. The reason for this emphasis is no mystery. Sexual attraction is sensational and immediate, requiring no thought or discernment but merely an appeal to a universal appetite. Therefore, it is a quick sell, and for that reason, it can be used to push everything from soap to cars to books, music, movies, and TV programs.

Our young people are greatly affected by this. They have been conditioned not to discern the difference between hormonally charged attraction and the deep, sacrificial love of couples like Della and Jim that puts the beloved first at all costs. Today the popular image of love consists of gazing into each other's eyes, romantic interludes, soft music, candlelight dinners, and caresses and kisses leading to earth-moving sex.

But reality has another side to it. Real love shows itself by putting up with snoring, nursing through illness, adjusting tastes in deference to the other, working out conflicts, cleaning up milk spills, changing dirty diapers, walking a crying infant at two in the morning, and stretching thin budgets. The dazzling sparkle of erotic attraction often blinds young people to these grimmer realities and lures them like sirens to the altar of disaster. Much of today's alarming divorce statistics can be traced to this blinding to the depths of love by the promise of unending romantic and erotic ecstasy. But when the stars in the eyes fade in the glare of morning daylight, the glamour of immediate attraction disappears, and the unsatisfied longing remains—the longing to be loved deeply and sacrificially. Only this kind of love affirms our worth. Without it, we feel of little value, and erotic sensations do not compensate.

The Necessity of Love

This need for deep, sacrificial love is basic to all of us. M. J. Rutter, director of Clinical Research at the Cincinnati Children's

Hospital Medical Center, cites the marked difference in children who are deprived of love early and those who are not. He compared kids raised in isolation from love in Romanian orphanages with those raised in loving homes. "Persisting cognitive and emotional defects" occurred much more frequently in abandoned infants as compared to those raised in nurturing environments. Furthermore, a study of English and Romanian adoptees revealed, "Toddlers who were removed from Romanian orphanages before the age of six months and then adopted by dedicated families in the United Kingdom showed a remarkable degree of catch-up despite severe developmental deprivation on arrival."[2] Love made the difference in their cognitive, emotional, and developmental health. Love is not an option; it is a necessity.

Family psychologist Kevin Leman cites a study of forty-nine different cultures throughout the world to show that the most violent ones were those in which displays of affection were rare in the home.[3] Love not only makes the world go round, it keeps the axis oiled so that it turns smoothly.

We believe that most parents love their children more than their own lives and would not hesitate to throw themselves in front of a train or donate their last kidney to save their child. But often that love is not apparent to the kids. Part of the reason is that in the frantic pace of their lives, parents seldom find the time to show it. In 63% of today's homes, both parents hold outside jobs. Kids living in these homes spend an average of 20% of their time alone. School activities, sports, homework, housework, church functions, working out schedules to get family members to all their events, and simple exhaustion all conspire to keep parents and kids from spending time together. As a result, family members get caught up in their own separate little worlds, and they begin to feel isolated from each other.

This sense of alienation can be even worse in broken homes, which are quickly becoming the norm in the United States. Almost half of American kids today have experienced the divorce of their parents. In divorced households, the single parent must do the work of two, intensifying the frantic pace that creates chaos even in two-parent homes. In such environments, there is little time even to think about demonstrating love in a tangible way.

Our need and longing for deep love is so overwhelming that when home love is dysfunctional or not apparent, kids will inevitably seek love outside the home. Their universal need for it cannot be denied. They will search for love wherever they can find it—in connections with friends, teams, clubs, gangs, and especially the opposite sex. Not all such outside connections are inherently unhealthy. In fact, many of them are desirable when there's a solid connection of love at home. As long as home is the reliable base and the other connections are satellites, our children feel secure.

But when love is not shown at home and young people search for it elsewhere, the danger is threefold: (1) Deep love is seldom found in those connections they make outside the home. (2) The cultural values of others will dominate your kids and control their thinking and choices. (3) Sexual attraction, beginning naturally and forcefully in adolescence, exerts a powerful, magnetic pull on kids. When the demonstration of love is lacking or poor at home, they easily confuse sexual attraction with the love they are missing. Sex seems to meet their deep need for love, and so they enter a one-dimensional relationship that is not sacrificial but the opposite. It is self-seeking, with each partner using the other as a means of achieving sensational feelings to compensate for a lack of love. These relationships are essentially hormonal, body-to-body only, and devoid of deep commitment to the other because they are focused on meeting the needs and desires of self.

The Need for a Father's Love

The failure of fathers in particular to demonstrate love in the home can leave their children feeling anchorless and unvalued. The lack of a father's love is often harder on girls than boys.

Johns Hopkins University researchers found that "young, white teenage girls living in fatherless families . . . were 60 percent more likely to have premarital intercourse than those living in two-parent homes."[4] Often in sexual relationships girls are looking for the love they miss from their father. They need to feel the security of being valued and cherished by a masculine figure, and if the father does not provide it, they search for a male who will. In their desperation to find intimacy, they resort to sexual relationships, confusing the intensity of sex with the intimacy of love. Then, the problem mushrooms when they keep using sex in a desperate attempt to hold partners who never had real love for them. In time, girls find that sensation does not replace devotion, but by then, the consequences are often devastating. Rather than increasing closeness and love, girls who resort to sexual relationships find increased loneliness when mere physical sex does not meet their emotional need to be valued and cherished in a deeply committed love. Even the physical health and self-image of girls lacking a father's love often suffers. A study of thirty-nine teenage girls suffering from anorexia nervosa showed that thirty-six of them shared a common trait: The lack of a close relationship with a father.[5]

Divorce has left many families without fathers. Other fathers become absent emotionally if not physically when they are sucked up into their careers. The consequences are far-reaching, not only for girls, but for any child reared without evidence of a father's love. Dr. Armand Nicholi's research shows that an emotionally or physically absent father contributes to a child's low motivation for achievement, inability to defer immediate gratification, low self-esteem, susceptibility to group influence, and juvenile delinquency.[6]

I had this fact demonstrated poignantly to me when I spoke at an outdoor youth rally at a high school in Phoenix, Arizona. Shortly after I began speaking, a group of punk rockers, their hair dyed all colors and gold chains hanging on their necks, walked up and hovered ominously at the edge of the crowd. I had been warned that this group might cause trouble. I kept my eyes on them as they just stood there as if daring me to say something worth listening to. When I ended my talk, I stepped down from the boulder that had served as my rostrum, and the husky young leader of the punkers ran right up to me and stood with his face inches from my nose. Most of the crowd could neither see nor hear what happened next. They couldn't see the tears on the young man's cheeks or hear him respectfully ask, "Mr. McDowell, would you mind giving me a hug?" Before I could raise my arms, the big punker hugged me like a bear, put his head on my shoulder, and sobbed like a baby in front of the whole school. I hugged him back, putting my whole heart into it. After a minute or more, he stepped back and explained, "My father never once hugged me or told me he loved me." In his own dramatic way, this young man made a strong statement about our universal need for a father's love.

Why is a father's love so important? It may be due partly to the law of supply and demand, especially in those remaining homes where the father is still the sole breadwinner. Fathers who work all day have little available time at home. In the eyes of children and young people, mothers seem made for love; her love is "a given," whereas fathers "bestow" love. Regardless of the reason, it's obvious that kids desperately need a father's love. Every boy needs a loving man in his life as a positive role model for manhood and relationships. Every girl needs a secure and loving relationship with a man who cherishes her—not for what he can get from her but simply for who she is—to make her feel immensely valued.

The Highest Kind of Love

The kind of love we most deeply need is not friendship, affection, or sexual love, though all of these are God-given and of immense value. Our deepest need is for the deepest kind of love, the love that underlies all the others, the *agape* love of the Bible, what

Lewis calls sacrificial love. This kind of love gives us the highest confirmation of our value—a love so strong that the one who loves values us more highly than his or her own possessions, comfort, health, or life. This was the kind of love that Jim and Della gave to each other in the O. Henry story. Their unhesitating willingness to give up their most valuable possessions for each other leaves little doubt that they would as quickly give up their own lives.

The movie *Saving Private Ryan* tells of a detail of World War II soldiers who are assigned the task of bringing home a private whose mother has already lost all her other sons in the conflict. In the expedition to find and save Private Ryan, most of the members of the rescue team are killed, including the commanding officer. Many years later, when the aged Ryan visits the grave of the officer, he breaks down in tears, asking his wife, "Have I lived a good life?" He knew that the price these men had paid placed a high value on him, and he wanted affirmation that his life had been worth their sacrifice.

In a perfect world—the world before the fall of Adam and Eve—such sacrifices would never be necessary. Sacrifices involve pain and deprivation, experiences not characteristic of a world of perfection. But in this fallen world, sacrificial love is often necessary to meet needs of others that can be met in no other way. And while we cannot desire that anyone would have to go through pain, loss, deprivation, or death for us, when they make such sacrifices, we find our value dramatically affirmed.

In Eden, the sense-dazzling romantic love of happy-ever-after eternal ecstasy that we crave was a reality. That kind of starry-eyed love could have lasted forever without the jarring need for sacrifice. The ravishing beauty of the earth and heavens gave ample evidence that God's love for Adam and Eve was all about delight and joy—the rich aromas on the caressing breezes, the sensational taste of all varieties of food, the delightful feel of fresh grass beneath their feet, the coolness of water on their skins, the fawning affection of the animals, the lavish colors and beauty of the trees, flowers, streams, and mountains, the complementary nature of their own bodies and personalities, and the bond of heart-pounding love between them. Everything in creation attested to the overwhelming love of the God who made them. And they gave that love back to him in the fullest measure possible.

But after the fall, the kind of love Adam and Eve experienced changed dramatically. Now they needed not merely an ecstatic sensational love that bestowed continual delights; they needed a love that would stay with them when delight faded and they became unlovable—a sacrificial love that would minister to their desperate need. And their need was indeed desperate. Without a love willing to sacrifice itself for them, their sin would doom them to eternal death. Thank God that his love was exactly that kind of love. God went beyond the ecstatic ideal he had intended for the man and woman and met their desperate need, sacrificing himself for their sin. And God's sacrificial love reaches all the way from Adam and Eve to each of us today. He loves you individually just as much as he loved Adam or Eve, and he sacrificed himself for you individually simply because he loves you too much not to address your deepest and most desperate need. As the apostle Paul tells us, "He gave himself for us to set us free from every sin" (Titus 2:14).

Our young people experience a compelling need for this kind of sacrificial love. This need reveals itself in a deep desire to be cherished, honored, and valued as a beloved person in the eyes of someone who focuses on them as highly important. Most young people haven't a clue that God loves them in just this way. If we want them to discover this highest kind of love that God has for them—sacrificial love that wills their best at any cost—we must show it in our behavior. This doesn't mean that we must run out and start looking for ways to die for them. It means that we show our willingness to put their needs ahead of our own whenever it is required. They must see sacrificial love in our treatment of them in order to help them understand that God loves them the same way. They need to see that we cherish them, honor them, love them, and value them highly in spite of their failures and shortcomings. How does that kind of love look when put into action? That's what we will explore in this section.

CHAPTER 11

How Christ Meets Our Need for Sacrificial Love

Everyone who knew Dan and Michelle said the same thing: they had never seen a married couple so happy and so in love with each other. The two did everything together. They played tennis, swam, attended concerts, took long walks in the park, and often had dinner by candlelight. It was obvious to all the young, upscale professional friends in their social circle that Dan and Michelle delighted in each other's company. Though they had been married for over a year, the honeymoon showed not the slightest sign of ebbing.

But just before their second anniversary, tragedy struck. One afternoon while Michelle was crossing a downtown street, a car hit her, and her injuries left her permanently paralyzed and brain damaged. She could still communicate by making sounds intelligible only to Dan, but she was now wheelchair-bound and could no longer feed or dress herself or take care of her personal needs. As a well-paid professional, Dan could afford to hire a nurse to be with Michelle while he worked. But her needs were such that he often had to leave his office and help the nurse tend to her. For a while, Dan's supervisors were sympathetic and tolerated these absences, but after a few weeks, their sympathy ran its course and he had to take a lower-paying job that gave him more flexibility. This meant moving into a smaller apartment and selling his Lexus and his boat. No longer could he socialize with his friends or find moments for recreation. He spent all his time tending to Michelle.

One evening a year after Michelle's release from the hospital, their old friends Ricky and Loni dropped by. Michelle sat slumped in her wheelchair in the kitchen as Dan fed soup to her with a spoon, gently asking her to open her mouth and close it on the spoon, then wiping away what ran down her chin. Her beauty was gone. She was extremely thin, and her once-mesmerizing eyes were dull and vacant, her useless hands drawn up like twisted claws. The only thing about her that looked like the old Michelle was her hair, which was neatly trimmed and combed to a lustrous sheen, obviously the work of her husband. When the feeding was done, Dan excused himself while he took Michelle to the bedroom and lifted her into her bed, and then he returned to visit with his friends.

"We came to invite you to go skiing with us next month," said Ricky.

"Thanks, Ricky. You know I appreciate it, but the answer is the same as for all the previous times you've invited me. I can't leave Michelle that long."

"That's what we want to talk to you about," Ricky cleared his throat and looked at Loni, who picked up her cue.

"We are worried about you, Dan," Loni said. "You are so tied down that you never get out and have fun any more." She looked at Ricky and swallowed before saying what they had come to say. "Uh, Dan, have you considered putting Michelle in a nursing home so you can get your life back?"

"No, of course not," replied Dan. "I could never do that to Michelle."

"She would hardly even know it," replied Ricky. "Rest homes today are not what they used to be. She would be cared for very well, and you wouldn't have to live like a monk in a monastery. You are burying yourself with all your talent and your bright future. If she could tell you, she would say the same thing. She wouldn't want to hold you back and be such a burden to you."

"She's not a burden; I love her," replied Dan.

"I know you do, and you could still love her. You could visit her as often as you like. You are young, Dan. You need more companionship than she can give you. This is not what you bargained for when you married. No one would blame you if you put her in a home. It's what most people would do."

"Look," said Dan, "when we married, we hoped for lifelong ecstasy. We hoped the romance and roses would bloom forever. But we didn't fall in love with romance and ecstasy; we fell in love with each other. We didn't take vows that we would love each other as long as the road was smooth and the lights were green. We made long-term commitments to love each other regardless. That's what I promised, and that's what I intend to do."

God's love for us is like Dan's love for Michelle. When he made us, he intended a relationship filled with continual ecstasy and delight. We are often told that the romantics among us are blinded to reality by the stars in their eyes and that romance is a passing feeling of the moment which will never last. But God did not intend for the romance of relationships ever to grow dim or die. All those wonderful romantic feelings that began with our teenage crushes and culminated in our wedding days are God-given, and he created love to be forever filled with such palpitating ecstasy.

But Adam and Eve's sin changed all that. When our primeval parents chose to focus on self rather than God, the romance and delight of love was spoiled by the intrusion of pain. Far from producing ecstasy, love now often brings on the need for the kind of sacrifice that Dan made for Michelle. And that's the kind of need that humanity's fall placed before God. Of course, we know how God met that need. He came down and sacrificed himself for us.

Why Would God Die for Us?

We can imagine God on his throne in heaven, looking sadly down on the ruined earth after Adam and Eve fell. Gabriel and Michael stand beside him, their angelic eyes following his forlorn gaze.

"Do you see what has happened," God said, slowly shaking his head. "The man and woman I created have ruined everything. They have rejected me and sided with the enemy."

"Yes, that is too bad," replied Gabriel, "and after all the effort you put into making them happy. Oh well, you tried. What more can you do?"

"The little ingrates!" said Michael, scowling. "Forget them! They are not worth any more of your time and attention. Let Satan have them, I say. After all, they're just creatures. You did fine without them before you made them, and you will do fine without them again."

"I'm going after them," said God, as if he hadn't heard a word the two angels said.

"Going after them?" asked Gabriel. "What do you mean? How will you do that? They have become rebels and traitors. They are doomed to death."

"I will go down and become one of them. I will live my life with them and take the death they deserve," answered God.

"What?" Michael was incredulous. "You would give up heaven and go live in that messed up world, with all its storms, droughts, earthquakes, heat, and cold; with all those flies and gnats buzzing around you all the time; with all the disease, accidents, and tragedies plaguing everyone's lives? Why would you do a thing like that?"

"Because I love them," said God. "They are worth it to me."

"They certainly don't look worth it," replied Gabriel. "Look at them! They've messed up your earth; they're blind to your love; they mistreat each other miserably, they're selfish, prideful, lustful, envious, deceitful, and hateful. What's the point in saving them? Why not wipe them out and start all over?"

"It's simple," said God. "I love them, and the thought of being without them for the rest of eternity just hurts me too deeply to express."

This scene is fictional, of course, but the love it describes is not. Even before Adam and Eve sinned, God determined in advance to do whatever it took to rescue us if we chose to turn away from him (Ephesians 1:4; 1 Peter 1:20). So, it meant death. That didn't matter. So, it meant a grueling, bloody, and agonizing death on an instrument designed for extreme torture. That didn't change a thing. One fact remained, and in the mind of God that fact was all that counted. We needed to be rescued from death, and whatever it took, he would do it in order to get us back.

When we say that Christ sacrificed himself for us, we are usually thinking of the pain and death he endured. And we are right to think that. But we often forget that the sacrifice involves not only what he endured, but also what he gave up. Before the incarnation, God was in his heaven, bonded in perfect harmony and love within his triune nature. God "had it all" in the most literal sense of the phrase. Nothing in the universe was lacking to him. There was no reason for his peace ever to change. Yet he chose to take the risk of creating humans and giving them the freedom to love or reject him. When they rejected him, he chose to leave all the wealth of the universe and become poor for our sake, even to the point of suffering brutal torture and death in a most cruel and painful way.

Why would God do this for messed-up creatures like you and me? The apostle Paul gives us the answer. "You know about the kindness of our Lord Jesus Christ. He was rich, yet for your sake he became poor in order to make you rich through his poverty" (2 Corinthians 8:9). Jesus gave up heaven and came to earth simply because he loved us. He loved us deeply—in human terms we might even say desperately. He cherished us and could not stand to lose us. We were worth more to him than all of heaven.

How could we bumbling humans possibly be worth all that to the God who created the universe? We don't know. But his enormous love is a mind-boggling fact that forces us to look at ourselves in a new way. We are worth something. We have value.

Though our value is not immediately apparent to each other because of the dirty crust of sin that covers us, God looks at us through the romantic lens of Eden and sees the beautiful creature he intended. Yet he also looks at us through the diagnostic lens of a physician and sees the deadly disease that we must be cured of. And because he loves us dearly, he is willing to take that deadly disease upon himself to save us from it.

There is nothing we could have done to earn such a love from God. It is a family thing. He saw us as parents see their own rebellious children who turn against them. We are his own creation, and as parents love the children they beget and bear, he loves us in spite of what we have done and in spite of the fact that our sin made us his enemies. Just as you ache and hurt for your children when they suffer pain and heartache, God aches and hurts for you. When sin inflicted death upon you, you couldn't come to him, so he came down to you and took your death so he could draw you back to him and give you life.

If you were to wear a price tag stating your worth, it would read: Jesus. The incarnation and sacrifice of Christ shows how much God loves you and how much he wants to reestablish that intimate relationship with you that he enjoyed with Adam and Eve. It shows how much he longs for us to live with him in unassailable joy and delight for all eternity.

CHAPTER 12

Modeling Sacrificial Love

Carl Morton was approaching puberty, and he had not been growing and developing physically like he should. Just before he turned thirteen, doctors put him through extensive tests and found a defect in his pituitary gland that would have to be corrected both surgically and medically or he would be dwarfed and deformed his entire life. Furthermore, the surgery had to be done immediately before he entered the critical stage of adolescence. The operation was highly specialized and enormously expensive, and the family would have to travel to a well-known clinic halfway across the nation to have it performed. They set up the date with the surgeon, Carl's father took his vacation, and the Morton family made plans to travel to the clinic.

At the last minute, the insurance company found a loophole in the policy that excluded such surgery from their coverage. The Morton family was devastated, but Carl's father refused to cancel the surgery. He negotiated with the clinic to work out a payment plan. As part of the agreement, the Mortons would sell their home and one of their cars to raise immediate cash. To make the heavy payments, they would cut out such luxuries as cable service, golfing, weekend trips to the seashore, and eating out on weeknights. Even with these stringent measures, their debt to the clinic would likely strap the Morton family budget for the rest of the parents' lives.

The delicate surgery was successful, but Carl would have to spend weeks at the hospital while the doctors monitored his medication. Meanwhile, the Mortons sold their home and moved into a smaller house. When Carl finally came home, he was greeted with a surprise party of several friends and relatives, complete with cake and gifts. As he sat at the table with the cake in front of him and his family and friends filling the room, tears welled up in his eyes. "I can't believe you feel like celebrating," he said, turning toward his father and mother. "Here you've had to sell your home, a car, give up lots of things most people take for granted, and go into debt for the rest of your lives just because you are stuck with a son who had a problem. And here you are smiling, hugging, and celebrating. How can you do that?"

Carl's father knew just what to say. "Oh, that's easy," he replied. "We can do this for you because it was done for us. You see, I was sick with a disease of sin, and Jesus Christ paid the cost of healing me. It cost him his home in heaven, but he didn't think twice. He wanted me well, and he would do whatever it took to get me there. And when I was healed, the angels were so happy that they threw a party in heaven. So, I'm just passing on what I have received. And I'm doing it for the same reason. He loved me too much to leave me with my disease. And that's just how I love you, Carl."

Without a word, Carl stood up and hugged his parents. Of course, by then all the women were sniffing and dabbing tissues at their mascara while the men suddenly found that a little piece of dust had just got in their eyes. But good old Uncle Orville, showing wisdom almost equal to that of his brother, said, "Okay, the sermon's over. Are we going to stand around and blubber or is someone going to cut that cake?" Everyone laughed and the celebration began.

That night in the silence of his room, Carl committed his life to Christ, and the next Sunday, he was baptized.

Just as Mr. Morton pointed out, the deep, sacrificial love that he and his wife had for their son clearly reflected the sacrificial love of Christ. And Carl picked up on the parallel. Because of the magnitude of his parents' sacrifice and their celebratory joy in his newfound health, he could not help but know that he was dearly loved and highly valued. He could see that he was the recipient of a twofold love. The love of his parents was really the love of Christ flowing through them. It was more love than he could comprehend, more than he could absorb. All he could do was respond by giving that love back by entering a relationship with the ultimate source of all love.

Sacrificial love, agape as it reads in the Greek, is the highest form of love. It is the kind of love that wills the well-being of the other above the well-being of self. Kids cannot help but know that they are valued highly and have great worth in the eyes of the one who demonstrates such a love. And if they are made aware of the ultimate source of such a love—that we as parents, teachers, or youth workers are passing on the kind of love that God gave us—they get the clearest picture that we can give them of the way God loves us.

Virtually all of us who are parents would make the kind of sacrifice for our children that the Mortons made for Carl. In fact, it's likely that all of us would go even further; we would sacrifice our health or even our lives for our sons and daughters. We've all heard of cases where a parent gave up a kidney for a child who would not survive without a transplant. And we've heard of cases in which parents threw themselves in front of cars, or drowned, or burned to death, or were killed by wild animals to save a child. Most of us would make these sacrifices readily, but few of us are called to take such extreme measures. So if our children need to see the agape love that God has for them demonstrated in our lives, how are we to show it?

Showing Sacrificial Love

While few of us are called on to sacrifice our lives, health, or fortunes for our kids, none of us escapes the need to make smaller, more continuing sacrifices. From the time your infant comes home from the hospital, your comfortable life is disrupted. You walk your crying baby at two o'clock in the morning, losing valuable sleep you will sorely miss the next day. Expensive jackets and suits will be ruined with a permanent burp stain on the shoulder. You will miss nights out with your friends because you need to stay home with the baby. You will spend evenings helping kids with homework or school projects instead of spending your free time on your favorite hobbies. You will teach your son to throw a football or your daughter to hit a softball even though it means giving up golfing with your buddies. You will give up that dream vacation to Europe and that new boat in order to put your son or daughter through college.

In some ways, these ongoing, smaller sacrifices can be more difficult to make than the big ones. You can pump yourself up and find the courage to make the big sacrifices and even feel a certain sense of grandeur and nobility about making them. But the little, mundane, ongoing things we must do and give up for our kids have no such glory, and they can sometimes become tedious and grinding. "Do I have to tie up yet another Saturday getting three kids to three different ball games?" "What! Yet another fee from Darla's university? They're going to nickel and dime me into bankruptcy!" "Here I am watching *Narnia* for the seventeenth time instead of watching the Cowboys on *Monday Night Football.*" "So Elyssa needs braces too. Well, it looks like we'll be driving the old Chevy for a couple more years." When you have kids the constant barrage of ongoing, everyday needs and little mundane duties that pull you away from what you would rather do may tend to wear you down. As Dr. Livingstone said of the dangers and difficulties he faced in the deepest jungles of Africa, "It wasn't the lions and tigers that bothered us; it was the gnats." You can find glory in slaying a lion but not in swatting a gnat. However, when you are driven by love, you will willingly take on whatever faces you for the well-being of your kids—lions, tigers, or gnats.

In almost any endeavor, the key to success is in the little, ongoing details. Some of the great battles in history lasted only minutes, but they were the result of hours upon hours of planning, tedious marching, endless practice with weaponry, coordinating and transporting food and supplies, cleaning and maintaining equipment, and hours or even days of simply waiting and watching. We read great novels that move us to the core, little thinking about the author staring at a blank page trying to begin the next chapter, making five or six starts before he gets traction, poring over the construction of each sentence, searching his thesaurus to find just the right word, endless revisions and rewrites, wrestling with proper grammar, proofing several times for consistency, spelling errors, and syntax.

In dealing with our kids, it's the tedious, ongoing, seemingly mundane sacrifices that demonstrate our love and give our kids an umbrella sense of being cherished and valued. Little children will not consciously appreciate what we do for them, though subliminally they will sense that they are loved. But as they grow, they will become more aware that what Mom and Dad do for them shows how highly valued they are. And through this ongoing sacrifice in the name of love, you demonstrate to them the nature of God.

Sensitive adults who know their young people intimately will understand their feelings and know their needs. They can show their love by being alert to opportunities for occasional sacrifices that may help their kids in lesser ways than protecting their health or survival. Sometimes what seems a small sacrifice to you may have huge meaning to your kids. Eighteen-year-old Derek was at the bathroom mirror nervously checking out his clothes and his hair before he left to pick up Kecia, his date for the senior prom. Kecia was one of the prettiest girls in high school, and he could hardly believe that she had said yes when he finally worked up the nerve to ask her. The only glitch to a perfect evening was his car, a twelve-year-old Honda four-door with several prominent dents and rust spots, a cracked windshield, no air-conditioning, and a hole in the muffler. Derek had planned to borrow his Dad's brand new Mercury Marquis until he found that his parents had a date to attend the opera the night of the prom. As embarrassing as it was, his old car would just have to do.

"Derek, may I come in?" his father's voice came from outside the bathroom door.

"Sure, Dad. It's open."

His father entered the bathroom, dressed in his best suit, ready to depart for the city opera. "Son, I was wondering if you would do me a big favor tonight," he said. "Your car is so much like the one I had when your mother and I were dating; I thought it would be nice to take her out in it just for old times' sake. Would you mind trading cars with me just for tonight?" He held up the keys to his new Mercury.

Instead of reaching for the keys, Derek reached for his dad, and hugged him for several seconds. "Thanks, Dad," he said, deep appreciation clearly showing in his eyes and voice. At that moment he knew that his dad meant more to him than any car.

From the father's point of view, this sacrifice was a small one. The worst thing he has to face is the disdainful look of the valet who parks the car at the theater, which will likely give him and his wife a good laugh. But from Derek's point of view, the sacrifice is enormous. It has saved him from what he thought would be serious embarrassment. And he cannot help but know that his parents love him when they are sensitive not merely to his serious needs, but even to his little felt needs. Like Jesus at the wedding feast at Cana, they went out of their way to save a loved one from humiliation. Even in their small but sensitive sacrifice, they demonstrated the nature of God to their son.

It's not uncommon for families to be called on to make sacrifices somewhere between the little things and the big, life-threatening ones. I (Tom) was privileged to know a couple at a church in Austin who grew up and married in a west Texas town where they had their family roots. Their second son was born deaf. In terms of economics and maintaining relationships with their extended family, it would have been better for them to remain in their hometown. But they pulled up stakes and moved to Austin where they could put their son in a special school for the hearing impaired. The entire family learned sign language and became experts at it. The father became a carpenter, taking mostly short-term jobs where he could find them. He didn't get rich, but he supported his family responsibly, and their deaf son grew up to be talented and productive, a fine Christian young man now holding a good job and happily married with children of his own.

I often had occasion to watch this family interact, and it was clear that the deaf son had an excellent relationship with his father. They worked hard together, they communicated well, and they joked with each other. The boy could not help but know he was highly cherished and deeply loved. His family had uprooted their lives because of him and rebuilt everything around his need.

When we sacrifice to meet our children's needs, they have little trouble understanding the sacrifice that Christ made for us. They can see the same kind of love in action in our treatment of them.

If a father finds that he has a dinner scheduled with an important client on the same evening his son's city league championship game will be held, it may seem like a tough call to reschedule the dinner. But if he does not reschedule it, his son will get the message. He is not an important element in his dad's life. He will not feel highly valued.

When parents are not involved in their kids' lives on a day-to-day basis, children will have trouble thinking the parents really love them deeply. But when it becomes obvious to your kids that you are giving up needs or even preferences to be with or do things for them, they will come to realize that they are important to you. The idea of sacrificial love is planted. A sense of value is established. Showing sacrificial love need not mean that parents must find ways to give up their lives for their kids. But when a father gives up a long-anticipated company trip to Florida he won as a reward for meeting sales goals in order to attend his daughter's piano recital, it's not hard for her to make the mental leap that he loves her more than he loves himself, and would even die for her.

Expressing Love

Our focus in this chapter is on how we demonstrate God's sacrificial love to our kids. But we want to veer a little aside to address an important, closely related subject: the importance of *expressing* your love to your children. While sacrificial *agape* love is the bedrock of your love for them, that love can seem cold and mechanical, based more on duty than on real love unless you express it overtly with ongoing verbal and physical affection. Kids need to see and hear your love displayed in a tangible way. When we show affection, it says to them, "I'm glad you are in my life. I delight in you. You mean much to me."

Many parents, fathers in particular, often find expressing affection awkward and difficult. Their own fathers, raised in the stoic, John Wayne culture of masculine self-sufficiency, may not have expressed affection to them. They have no model for fatherly affection, and thus they have trouble showing it. Fathers who carry such emotional baggage must work through it for the sake of their children.

One solution is to look for role models. I grew up without experiencing any kind of affection from my own father, and would likely have known nothing about how to express it had it not been for my close friend, Dick Day. When I first met Dick, I was a young, single seminary student while he was in the same seminary a little ahead of me. He was married with four children. Our friendship became so close that I soon became a virtual member of his family. I was highly impressed with how Dick and Charlene treated each other and their children. Their relationships were rich and rewarding, full of mutual respect, fun, laughter, and hugs. From them I learned much about treating people with love and respect—and I even learned to hug! In Dick Day I saw a clear, concrete model of the kind of father I wanted to be when I had my own family. I owe much to Dick, and no doubt my family does as well.

One of the first principles I learned from Dick was how important it is to your kids that you show affection to your wife or husband within the walls of the home. Often we see people who are courteous, patient, and kind to their spouses at church or social functions. But it all disappears, and they drop the façade of kindness to become self-centered ogres when they walk through the door of their home. We must not shed our love and courtesy when we relate to our families. Those in our homes are the ones who mean the most to us. They are the ones we love more than our own lives. We must show that love by giving them the best of our courtesy, good will, patience, and good humor. We must show love in the home in every word and every action.

What Dick Day did for me shows how other adults in the lives of young people can be a positive influence to fill in where parental love and affection is lacking. When youth pastors or teachers see evidence of a lack of love for kids in a given home, they can be alert to opportunities to supply a sure-to-be-missing sense of value and acceptance. This need is especially strong in kids living in troubled or broken homes. Often their craving to feel valued and affirmed is overpowering. And they are always looking for affirmation of their worth and ways to meet that need to be cherished and loved. Showing love and acceptance to them is one way to rebuild in them a sense of self-worth and help them to know that they are loved even when evidence of it is missing in the home.

It is more than sad when kids do not see love modeled in their homes. Modeling love is by far the most effective way to teach one to love. We once had a plaque in our home that read, "The most important thing a father can do for his children is to love their mother." Parents are the models for love in the home (Ephesians 6:1–4). Genuine love demonstrated between a husband and wife gives children a strong feeling of security. They see the home as a solid, intact unit because they see evidence of the glue that holds Mom and Dad together in the affection they display for each other. Love flows from the center of the home and enfolds the children, just as love flows from the center of the triune nature of God and enfolds us. And it's not just the words and hugs, but the way couples treat each other all the time as a matter of course— the thoughtfulness, help, encouragement, compliments, and humor. "In honor preferring one another" is the rule for showing love to everyone, especially those to whom we are closest.

Parents need to express love verbally, not only to their spouses but to their children as well. We macho fathers must learn to say "I love you" without awkwardness and embarrassment. We know it's as hard to do as swallowing raw oysters, but you can do it if you put your mind to it. Practice in front of a mirror if you must. Open your mouth and force your reluctant tongue to form those three difficult words until you can do it without blushing. Then put what you have learned into practice. Tell your kids at least occasionally how much they mean to you and how they add joy to your life.

And while you are at it, don't overlook the need to express affection physically. A loving touch strengthens the emotional connection. It's a kind of nonverbal language that also says "I love you." Hugs, pats on the arm, and an occasional playful tussle will do much to say, "I am delighted to have you around." With boys, fathers can use that old manly fist-to-shoulder gesture. Even teenagers need affection shown physically. But be discreet about when you show it. Don't embarrass them by getting too mushy in front of their peers.

When my (Tom's) older daughters, Sherrinda and Audra, were teenagers, they developed scoliosis and had to wear klunky metal and leather braces for nearly two years to help their backs grow straight. The braces could not be hidden; the collar fit around their necks, and the forms of the vertical bars were visible through their shirts and blouses. During this difficult time for them, I developed a habit of feigned boxing with them, punching them in the stomach where they were well-protected by a metal bar of the brace. The playful sparring said, "Your brace does not change anything about you. You are the same daughter I have always loved and enjoyed having in my life. We can still have the same kind of fun we've always had." The simple gesture showed affection, good humor, and complete acceptance of the girls inside the braces.

Ultimately, showing affection to your kids gives them a sense of security and confidence. They feel loved, cherished, and protected. It also does much to turn them into affectionate adults by modeling to them how affection is communicated. But one of the greatest benefits to parents is that showing affection to your kids will cause them to show affection to you. They will be more affectionate because your love will be so visible that it will activate their desire to reciprocate. They will also be more open with you and more receptive to your guidance if they are convinced that you love them deeply.

The Vow at the Crib

We end this chapter with a word to new fathers. Shortly after your newborn child has been brought home from the hospital, we recommend that you choose a night to engage in a brief, private ceremony. On that chosen night when everyone else is asleep, get out of your bed and tiptoe into the nursery where your newborn is sleeping in the crib. Look down on that innocent, helpless, and precious little creature you helped bring into the world and utter a solemn, heartfelt vow and a fervent prayer. Promise before God that you will dedicate yourself utterly and selflessly to your child's well-being, that you will place his or her welfare, safety, health, and happiness above your own, and that your own happiness and desires will be subordinate to the happiness and well-being of your son or daughter. Then pray that you will be successful in giving back to God this life that he has given to you for care and safekeeping. When you are finished, tiptoe back to your bed, put your arms around your wife, and go to sleep.

Such a vow and prayer could be a turning point for your own life. You will have made a Christlike commitment of love to sacrifice yourself for another cherished being. It will be a milestone of your own spiritual maturity that you can look back on when you are in the middle of that seemingly never-ending need to keep giving of yourself. It will remind you of what is important in your life. And in modeling selfless, sacrificial love, you will be taking a solid step toward becoming more like Christ so that you can reflect him to others, especially to your precious child.

PART II

SECTION 4

God Relates to Us Continually

CHAPTER 13
Our Need for a Continuing Relationship

Fourteen-year-old Jeffrey stood on his driveway and lobbed his basketball toward the netless hoop mounted over the garage door. The ball soared through the goal without touching the peeling backboard or the rusting rim as it did more than half the times Jeffrey shot. He retrieved the ball and was dribbling it on the cracked concrete when he heard a car door shut in the driveway across the street. He turned to see his friend Trevor getting into the car with his dad. They were going to the arena to watch the Knicks play. Jeffrey waved and then turned away and shot again. The ball bounced off of the rim and landed on the weedy lawn. Jeffrey picked it up and sat on the porch step, staring at the cracks in the sidewalk before him.

He hoped his next dad would be like Trevor's. Trevor had never had but one father, but what a dad he was! He took Trevor to ballgames, movies, and fishing. He practiced shooting goals with him almost every afternoon and even took him on an annual camping trip in the mountains. Jeffrey had had three dads already, and he was sure that it wouldn't be long before his mother brought home another.

The first dad he could remember had not been all that great. He hardly had anything to do with Jeffrey, who was often left with babysitters while the couple went out in the evenings. Even when they were home, Jeffrey was usually sent to bed early so that the two adults could be alone. His second dad was a little better. He treated Jeffrey well enough when he was home, but he had a large sales territory and was on the road most of the time. Still, when he did come home, he brought Jeffrey great gifts and sometimes took him to the park and once even to the zoo. His third father, whose name was Brad, was the best. He played ball with Jeffrey, took him to ballgames, fishing, and swimming. He even installed the basketball goal above the garage and taught Jeffrey how to play the game. But after a while, his mom and Brad had started fighting, and finally Brad left. He had been gone for over a year now, and Jeffrey missed him greatly. Jeffrey's mother had brought home two or three men since, but Jeffrey hadn't cared much for any of them. He hoped this time Mom would find someone like Trevor's father, who liked to watch the Knicks play.

Jeffrey's story is not unusual. Over half the kids in America have experienced breakups in their homes, and many of them have had serial "fathers." The damage this does to children is almost incalculable. It deprives sons and daughters of any sense of loving, permanent, intimate relationships with one parent, and it often damages their relationship with the remaining one. Divorcing parents often justify going their separate ways, saying, "It's much better for the kids that we split up so they won't be brought up in a household of constant tension and fighting." This is nothing but bald rationalization. Statistics show that very few traumas devastate children as much as the divorce of their parents. According to the American Academy of Matrimonial Lawyers, "Only acts of war and the events of natural disasters are more harmful to a child's psyche than the divorce process."[1] Divorce has an affect on children that, according to journalist Tim Rotheisler, "can be 'worse than a parent's death.' Divorce is consistently associated with juvenile emotional disorders, crime, suicide, promiscuity and later marital breakup."[2] In almost every case, children did much better in homes where parents who almost divorced chose to stick it out for the sake of the children. Children can endure almost anything better than the destruction of a vital relationship that is meant to endure.

Some children never get over the side effects of destroyed parental relationships. They come to feel that they can never depend on any relationship to be permanent. It makes them wary of commitment and skeptical of promises. In any relationship they enter, they often feel an underlying fear that it will not last;

eventually, the other person will walk away. Often this feeling causes them to pull back on their own commitment, fearing to put their all into the relationship and, therefore, reserving part of themselves against hurt.

Children and young people often wonder about themselves when a father or mother leaves the home. They don't always see the breakup as simply between the parents; they feel they have been abandoned as well. A son or daughter will often assume that there must be something unlovable about himself or herself, or the parent would not have left. They question their own worth and begin to feel that they have traits that make them unlovable. "What is there about me that made me so easy to abandon?" they ask. But in spite of these questions about themselves, and in spite of their mistrust of relationships, one thing they will not give up—their desire and longing for a permanent, intimate, ongoing relationship with someone who finds them worth loving and worth being with.

The experience of a friend demonstrated one effect that the lack of permanent relationships with adults can have on kids. He and his wife adopted four siblings, ranging in age from eighteen months to nine years. The four children had spent most of their lives shuffled among several foster homes. What my friend did not anticipate was how easily these children would take up with any adult who came even casually into their environment. However, they would not bond deeply with anyone—not even with him or his wife, much to their grief. The children had acquired what psychologists call Random Attachment Syndrome (RAS). They would attach easily to any adult but deeply to none. The syndrome was more pronounced in the older siblings.

The reason these children developed RAS was no mystery. It was a coping mechanism, an automatic psychological defense against hurt or abandonment brought on by their life of being handed off from one household to another. This condition was not only disappointing to my friend and his wife, who longed for a deep, lasting bond with their newly acquired family, it was loaded with danger. The children could be led or enticed all too easily into attachments that would be harmful to them. And unless they overcame their RAS, deep, satisfying, long-term commitment would be difficult for them to achieve.

Why We Need Relationships

The loss or lack of solid, enduring relationships inflicts serious problems on our kids. The reason, as we have stated many times in this book, is simply that we are created for relationship. Therefore, when vital relationships are missing from our lives or when they go awry, an integral facet of our being is thwarted and our entire psychological and spiritual makeup is certain to malfunction.

Adam and Eve were created not only with a need for a horizontal relationship with others like themselves, but also for a vertical relationship with God. He created within them a vacancy designed to be filled with his own Spirit—a relationship that was meant never to end. Thus intimate and permanent relationships characterized the nature and purpose of their being. Adam and Eve could not be what they were intended to be without these relationships both with each other and with God.

When the seventeenth-century Anglican poet-clergyman John Donne wrote, "No man is an island," he merely recognized the truth of what God had said before he created Eve: "It is not good for the man to be alone" (Genesis 2:18).[3] We are interconnected with relationships that enfold us from birth to death, and these relationships are vital to our well-being. We cannot live without relationship. Felons who were isolated for months in medieval prisons went insane. While today's prisons are more humane, the punishment modern prisoners dread most is solitary confinement, where they are shut off from contact with all other human beings. We need each other. We cannot do without each other. This need for relationship is a basic component to our humanity.

Because we are created with this need for relationship, we constantly seek to be part of some community. We join clubs, bowling leagues, and churches; we find golfing buddies and couples or families with whom we can go out to dinner or see movies. The old sitcom *Cheers* was popular at least in part because it played to our need to fill a place in a community, the bar in the show being a place where "everybody knows my name." Our kids play sports, establish circles of friends, join gangs, or latch onto boyfriends or girlfriends because they are seeking relationships.

But mere superficial connections do not satisfy our need for relationship. We can survive on such connections, but not thrive. We need more than those perfunctory greetings and handshakes or coffee break interactions we find at the church assembly or at work. Such cursory and shallow social encounters leave us feeling alone in a crowd. Chatting about weather, work, shopping, and sports is not enough. We all long for and need deep relationships where our hearts are intertwined with others. We need relationships in which we can safely bare our souls, knowing and understanding the other person intimately. We want enduring, unconditional relationships with others. We want assurance that in spite of our faults, weaknesses, and failures, they will always be there—always available, and always reliable.

One of the best-known examples of such a relationship is one that we find in the Old Testament: that of the Moabite girl Ruth with her mother-in-law, the Jewish widow Naomi. When their husbands died, these grieving women faced a dark and uncertain future. Naomi thought her best course was to return to her homeland Israel and find help from her own people. She encouraged her young daughter-in-law to stay in Moab and remarry. But the girl had come to love her mother-in-law deeply, and her reply remains even today an ideal expression of commitment to permanent relationship: "Don't force me to leave you. Don't make me turn back from following you. Wherever you go, I will go, and wherever you stay, I will stay. Your people will be my people, and your God will be my God. Wherever you die, I will die, and I will be buried there with you. May the Lord strike me down if anything but death separates you and me" (Ruth 1:16–17).

The rest of Ruth's story is just as impressive as her declaration of commitment. She gleaned in the fields of Judah for food for both Naomi and herself, and she took all her mother-in-law's advice on finding the right husband. As a result, Ruth wed a responsible, upstanding man who took care of both her and Naomi, giving them happiness in the relationship of a family. Somehow Naomi was able to draw such a love from her daughter-in-law that the girl committed to a lifelong relationship with her, showing us that the generation gap is not an automatic thing if adults take care to treat younger people with love and respect.

In the movie, *The Fellowship of the Ring*, the first of three based on Tolkien's literary epic *The Lord of the Rings*, the hobbit gardener Samwise Gamgee commits himself to be the companion and guardian of the hobbit hero Frodo. Frodo is on a perilous quest to destroy the ring of power, which is the only way Middle Earth can be saved from an encroaching evil. As Frodo begins to see how the power of the ring is destroying the fellowship, he decides to slip away and complete the quest on his own. But Samwise catches up with him and will not let him go on alone. He will not be deterred in spite of the impossible odds, declaring to his dear friend, "I made a promise, Mr. Frodo, a promise: 'Don't you leave him, Samwise Gamgee.' And I don't mean to."

Both in history and in story, such examples of committed relationships warm and inspire us. They picture something vital to the completion of our being, something we all hunger for. And when we are deprived of it, we feel isolated, incomplete, and disconnected. We long to have someone in our life like Ruth or Samwise who places such a value on us that that he or she will commit unconditionally to a never-ending, utterly dedicated relationship.

Such relationships are vital because they validate us. They give us assurance that we have value—that our existence has meaning and our lives have purpose. To have another who desires your company, who enjoys your personality, who wants to explore your mind and heart, who cares what you think and how you feel, who wants to protect you from pain and harm, and who seeks you out and wants to be with you gives you a powerful sense of worth. You know you have value simply because you can see that value reflected in the heart of another. Relationships validate us by allowing us to see the effect of our lives on the lives of others.

Young People Need Adult Relationships

One of the most miserable experiences a human being can endure is loneliness. In my ministry, I often encounter young people who experience devastating loneliness, some of it expressed in letters that break my heart. Here is one that's typical of hundreds more much like it:

> I am so lonely I can hardly stand it. I want to be special to someone, but there's no one who cares about me. I can't remember anyone touching me, smiling at me, or wanting to be with me. I feel so empty inside. It's like I have this heavy heart and this burden upon my back, but I don't know what it is. There is something in me that makes me want to cry, and I don't even know what it is.

Reading such a letter makes *me* want to cry. Sadly, the girl who wrote it had no one in her life to whom she felt special. She had no relationship to make her feel that she was valued or that her life had importance. And she is only one of millions of young people out there just like her. These are not only kids from broken homes or disadvantaged families where the parents must work multiple jobs to maintain the bare necessities. They are from every kind of environment, even respectable, middle-class Christian homes.

We often don't recognize the pain these young people bear because they learn to hide it well. Every morning when they get out of bed and put on their clothes and their jewelry, they also put on their masks. They wear these masks to appear assured and self-confident while inside they are desperately hoping they won't fall off the high wire. They go off to school, their clubs, their sports, their studies, their boyfriends or girlfriends, hoping to find themselves, or if they can't find themselves, perhaps to lose themselves.

But most of them are neither finding themselves nor losing themselves. They are finding that they are stuck with a self that they cannot understand and have no one to help them discover just who they are. And the search becomes so desperate that it inflicts deep hurt and frustration.

As a result, many of our young people hoard a silent anger inside, and they don't know why. Underneath it all, they feel the pain of loneliness even though most of their day is spent among people. They are with many people, but they have no solid, lasting relationships with any of them that they can depend on to be deep and permanent. They find no sense of personal worth because no one seems to want to connect with them intimately on a continuing basis. So the despair simmers and builds.

We as adults have the first responsibility of supplying committed relationships for our young people. Adult relationships are necessary to model maturity and give them a sense of security while they explore and discover themselves and their world. They desperately need such relationships. They may not act like it. They may seem to disdain adult values and attitudes, but it's merely part of the mask they wear. They wear this mask partly because they think most adults don't understand or trust them and partly because they want to seem competently in control of their lives. But beneath the mask is a kid who feels that his or her life is spinning out of control. With almost daily advances in technology and communication, modern culture is changing so fast that the current generation has trouble finding solid ground under their feet. The foundation seems to be shifting all the time, and they cannot feel the unshakeable absolutes that give them confidence in their actions and decisions. Deep inside, they long for you to see through the mask and reach out to them. They need and even want the security and stability of adult relationships to help them find the absolutes that will give them a sense of solidity. Caught up in the swirl of an ever-changing world, they hardly even know who they are, and they need adults who have their feet on the ground to enter their world and help them figure it out.

This need gives adults an opening to enter into relationships with young people and to show them the ultimate relationship that will provide a solid foundation for rebuilding a solid faith. But in our attempt to rebuild absolutes and begin a spiritual formation process, it's all too easy for us to make the common mistake we mentioned earlier in this book: that of relying too heavily on rules. "Just obey the rules we give you, and you will avoid the pitfalls waiting out there in this avaricious, materialistic, sex-saturated, self-gratifying, predatory culture." That is true enough as far as it goes, but they need more from us than mere rules. Adults who have little time for their kids often use rules as a substitute for relationship. They throw their kids a list and get on with their own pursuits, thinking the rules will be there even though they can't be. But when the kids grow even more distant and furtive, finding ways to gratify their wants behind the backs of adults, parents or teachers wonder where they went wrong. Didn't they do their duty by their kids in giving them the right principles for living? Why the backlash?

The answer is simple. Rules without relationship lead to rebellion. The rules are important and necessary, but without relationship, your young people will see them as merely your attempt to do your job and discharge your responsibility for them. They need to know that you will their good because you love them, not because it is your duty. They need to see that they are important enough in your life that you are willing to expend the time and energy to make a connection in relationship.

When a loving, ongoing relationship is established between an adult and a young person, adults usually find that they have less need to enforce rules. Kids start obeying from the attitude of "want to" rather than "have to" because relationship is reciprocal. The young person will want to maintain it as much as the adult and will tend to obey the rules out of love rather than fear of consequences. As the apostle John tells us, "No fear exists where love is. Rather, perfect love gets rid of fear" (1 John 4:18).

When adults fail to provide solid relationships with their young people, the need for relationship does not go away. It is too strong to deny, and kids will seek the relationship they long for in other places. Occasionally, this search produces happy results as when the young person finds a good friend of the same gender and of high character. But more often this is not the case. Because of their immaturity, kids seeking relationships do not readily see the pitfalls. Driven by need, they often become desperate and clingy in their outside relationships, making them vulnerable to predatory peers who will sense their desperation and use them for their own selfish purposes. Or they will fall into relationships with peers who share the same desperation, causing both parties to be grasping and self-seeking to get their own needs met.

Francine was shocked when she met her sixteen-year-old daughter Amber's new boyfriend. His head was shaved except for a spiked strip along the top, dyed orange. He wore a thin black moustache and goatee, all black clothing, rings in his ears and eyebrows, and hideous tattoos covered both arms. He seemed sullen and talked little, and when he did speak, his English was atrocious and his breath reeked of cigarette smoke. As a high school dropout, he had held several jobs in the past few months, and his current job was unloading trucks at an auto parts warehouse. Francine came down hard on Amber and forbade her to go with "that disgusting creature" again. But she had since learned that Amber had been slipping around and meeting him while Francine is at work. She wished her husband was home to help deal with his daughter, but his job kept him on the road three weeks of every month. And when he was home, paperwork, house repairs, and golfing—his only recreation—kept him too busy to be bothered.

It is clear that Amber was on the brink of disaster. If her parents had established an intimate relationship with her from childhood, the girl would not have been so desperately reaching in any direction for the relationship that she was missing at home. Her parents were harried with an overworked schedule, and perhaps they thought that it could not be avoided. But they needed to realize that their daughter was their first priority, and they needed to find a way to commit to a relationship with her in which they could learn what made her tick—her dreams, her strengths, her weaknesses, and her deepest needs. Once they established such a relationship with her, they would be able to model what an intimate relationship should look like while guiding her toward appropriate relationships with others and with Christ.

The Need for a Lasting Relationship

Perhaps the severest emotional pain we ever feel is the loss of a deep relationship. It was in defense against such pain that my friend's four adopted children developed Random Attachment Syndrome—superficial relationships with many people without letting any of them get so deep it would hurt them when the relationship ends. Deep relationships are so vital to us that when they are broken we experience grief. Even moving from one city to another causes a real sense of grief because it means relationships that we had come to depend on with people we love can no longer be the same. When a friendship is broken, we grieve. When a teenager is jilted, his or her world caves in. It hurts even worse when we grow into adulthood, and even worse yet when the parting destroys a marriage.

Many of our relationships last a lifetime, and those of us who are blessed with such should thank God daily. Eventually, however, all earthly relationships will end. A marriage relationship that lasts "till death do us part" is a wonderful blessing, but eventually death will force the parting. Therefore, all human relationships ultimately fail to fulfill that longing for permanence that is built into every one of us.

The chorus from an oldie song hit expressed sadness and perplexity at the alarming rate of broken marriages: "So what's the glory in living? Doesn't anybody ever stay together any more? And if love never lasts forever, tell me, what's forever for?"[4] The song asked an excellent question to which God has a ready answer. Forever is made for permanent, loving relationships. Only in God can we find the promise of a relationship that literally will never end. Only in him can we find a love that is truly eternal. He created us for a loving and joyous relationship with him that would last throughout all eternity. Christ came to earth to give us a way to reestablish that relationship with God. After he cleared the way, God gave us his Holy Spirit to live in us, making the relationship permanent. In the next chapter, we will explore what this permanent relationship looks like.

CHAPTER **14**

How Christ Meets Our Need for a Continuing Relationship

W hile Jesus was on earth, his disciples thought they had discovered heaven. In their relationship with him, they had found everything they could hope for. They were loved and fulfilled, and their lives had been given purpose. Just being with Jesus was to experience feelings, thoughts, and dreams unimagined before he came into their lives. Being perfect himself and understanding others perfectly, he could relate to them perfectly, giving them his best and drawing from them their best. The feeling expressed by the two men who met Jesus on the road to Emmaus was no doubt typical of many: "Were not our hearts burning within us while He was speaking to us on the road, while He was explaining the Scriptures to us?" (Luke 24:32, NASB). Jesus was the perfect satisfaction of their need for a committed relationship.

But after Jesus was tried and executed, these disciples were devastated. They thought this perfect relationship had ended forever. They grieved; they were depressed; they lost courage; they didn't understand what was happening. They hunkered down in hiding and struggled to come to terms with their loss, but then they heard the incredible report from the women who had been to the tomb: Jesus had come to life again. When this report turned out to be true, they were elated beyond comprehension. They could pick right up where they left off. The relationship could continue. And since this amazing man had defeated death, now the permanent, never-ending relationship they all longed for would become reality. We can only imagine their unbounded ecstasy as their minds burned with thoughts and ideas and possibilities they had never before considered.

But these poor disciples had one more shock ahead of them. After the resurrected Jesus had been among them for forty days, he gave them a charge to teach and spread abroad all they had learned of him. Then "he was taken to heaven. A cloud hid him so that they could no longer see him" (Acts 1:9). Jesus had earlier tried to prepare these men for the fact that he would be leaving them, but they could not come to terms with the thought because it overwhelmed them with sadness (John 16:5–6). They thought it meant the end of their incredible relationship with him. However, Jesus explained, "It's good for you that I'm going away. If I don't go away, the helper won't come to you. But if I go, I will send him to you" (John 16:7). So after Jesus ascended to heaven, the disciples did not despair as they had after he was crucified. Instead, "The disciples worshiped him and were overjoyed as they went back to Jerusalem" (Luke 24:52). Jesus had promised that their relationship with God would continue, but this time, he would come to them in the form of "the helper" who would not only be *with* them but also *in* them. Thus he promised them a relationship with God even closer and more intimate than they had enjoyed with Jesus while he was on the earth (John 14:17). It was not to be merely a one-to-one relationship, but one-*in*-one.

When the apostles and a few other disciples returned to Jerusalem after Jesus' ascension, they met together continually with about 120 believers, praying and encouraging one another for ten days until the day of Pentecost arrived. On that day, they were meeting together as usual when the spectacular events we described in chapter three occurred. The Holy Spirit came to these disciples in a brilliant and resounding display of fire and wind (Acts 2:2–4). The Holy Spirit of God was the helper Jesus had promised. On that day, God came to live permanently within the spirits of each of the disciples, and from that day forward, he has come into the life of every believer who commits himself or herself to Christ.

With the return of the Holy Spirit, God gave back to humanity what Adam and Eve had lost in Eden. The Spirit of God came down to fill the empty space left in our spirits by the fall, thus restoring to us the intimate relationship with God that had been lost to humanity. We again became what we were created to be— bearers of the life of God.

The incarnation of Christ was necessary to pave the way for the Holy Spirit to return. By his crucifixion, Jesus paid the price for sin and removed our guilt, making us clean so that God could renew the relationship. God could then come to us in the person of the Holy Spirit. Jesus could not simply stay and maintain the intimate relationship with every believer on earth because he had become a man, limited in space and time by the fact that he inhabited a body just like any human. For God to have his Spirit living in us, Jesus had to leave and allow God to come down in a spiritual form that could inhabit each one of us.

Becoming "Little Christs"

When Jesus became a man, for the first time since Adam sinned God had a human being walking on earth who behaved exactly like a human should. God had a human body on earth in whom he could live and express his nature. When Jesus ascended back into heaven, he gave us the privilege of replacing him, of becoming what he was—bodies on earth in whom God can live and express his nature. Essentially, when the Spirit of God enters us, we become "little Christs." We show God's likeness to those who are not yet Christian by drawing them into the same loving relationship that we experience. Thus we fulfill the charge that Jesus gave to his disciples before he ascended to heaven: "But when the Holy Spirit has come upon you, you will receive power and will tell people about me everywhere" (Acts 1:8, NLT).

The Restoration of All Things

Though God's plan for redemption is centered on his love for us, the scope of it is much broader than just reestablishing his relationship to humankind. He ultimately intends to restore all things to their original creation ideal. We've explained how when man and woman fell in Eden, they dragged nature down with them, damaging the environment and inflicting pain and suffering on all the creatures of the earth. Adam was meant to be the lord of the earth, but when he fell from created perfection, he forfeited his lordship to Satan (Luke 4:6; Ephesians 6:12; 1 John 5:19). When Satan took over, he ravaged the earth with death, pain, and evils of all kinds. When Christ returns his final victory will include the restoration not only of us, but also of all things in nature to their original creation ideal. The natural world was created to be our home, and God doesn't intend to let a malevolent creature like Satan have the victory of ruining forever what God pronounced to be good and created for our enjoyment. As Paul explains, "All creation anticipates the day when it will join God's children in glorious freedom from death and decay" (Romans 8:21, NLT).

The God Who Loves Us

The loving sacrifice of Christ and the presence of the Holy Spirit in our lives demonstrate the heart of a God intent on restoring all things to what he designed originally—a perfect relationship with his creation lived out in a perfect world. Our God is the God of redemption, relationship, and restoration. The very essence of his heart is love so intense that he wants companionship with his creation in an environment that delivers nothing but joy, happiness, and harmony. This picture of God is altogether different from that which many people seem to carry in their minds. He is not a stern and distant judge, looking down on us with a solemn, stony expression and checking our behavior against his law book. The sacrifice of Jesus and the coming of the Holy Spirit show us clearly that this picture of God is dead wrong. He is not looking down on us with righteous disgust; he longs to be with us. He wants to be our companion.

The life of Jesus on earth shows this to be true. He was utterly relational. He was continually with people. He had friends. He loved, he cared, he hurt with people, and he laughed with people. (Yes, Jesus had a sense of humor. He told stories about such things as people gulping down whole camels and running around with logs hanging from their eyes.) Jesus showed that God wanted to be with us and enjoy our company.

The Holy Spirit shows the same thing even more intimately. God not only wants to be with us, he wants to be *in* us. He wants to go with us wherever we go—to work, to the ball game, to the theater, to church, on vacation. As he did with Adam and Eve in Eden, God wants to take walks together with each of us and discuss the day's events. He delights in our company and longs for us to delight in his. As Paul told us, "For we know how dearly God loves us, because he has given us the Holy Spirit to fill our hearts with his love" (Romans 5:5, NLT).

It is possible even in this fallen world to develop a friendship with God. Abraham did it. He had such a close relationship with God that he was called God's friend (James 2:23). Moses had such a relationship with God that he and God were constant companions. We are told that "the Lord would speak to Moses personally, as a man speaks to his friend" (Exodus 33:11).

"Well, of course," you may say, "that was Abraham and Moses, giant heroes of the faith, not plain, common people like you and me." It's good that we admire these men who lived such godly lives, but we do them an injustice by putting them too high on a pedestal. In terms of their humanity, they were no more and no less than you and I. As the saying goes, "they put their pants on one leg at a time." (Or maybe more appropriately, they put their robes on one arm at a time.) Just like you and me, they struggled with temptations. They had to make human choices in the face of those temptations just exactly as you do. They did not become heroes of the faith because they had any exceptional advantage before God, but only because they made the right choices.

We can see a good picture of this friend-like relationship with God in the classic movie, *Fiddler on the Roof*. The Jewish milkman Tevye keeps a running dialog with God as he works his milk route, discussing his problems, telling God what's going on in the village and in his family, asking for blessings, commiserating over difficulties, and even laughing and quoting Scripture to him. It is the kind of relationship any one of us can develop. God is eager to be close to you. As James wrote, "Come close to God, and he will come close to you" (James 4:8).

Not long ago, God and I (Tom) shared a joke together. The joke was on me, but that didn't make it less funny. My wife and I were living in Nashville and taking a driving vacation to visit family in Dallas and Houston. On part of this trip, I would have my wife, my daughter, and two grandchildren in the car with me. Then I would leave them all in Dallas and drive back to Nashville alone. Having a fear of car trouble while I had so many passengers to be responsible for, I prayed what was, I suppose in retrospect, a somewhat silly prayer. I prayed, "If I must have car trouble, let it be on the part of the trip when I am driving alone." Well, God answered my prayer. I delivered my precious passengers safely in Dallas and headed back toward Nashville alone. While I was cruising along on Interstate 40 about halfway between Memphis and Nashville, my right rear tire blew out. I pulled over to change it, and as I hoisted the spare out of the trunk, I felt the almost tangible presence of God looking over my shoulder. And strangely, I felt that he was laughing.

For a moment I didn't get the joke, but then it hit me. It was as if God was saying, "Well, I answered your prayer, didn't I, Tom?" Yes, he had answered my prayer—just exactly as I had asked it. It was as if he was saying, "Why did you pray such a limited prayer? Why didn't you ask for my protection on your entire trip?" I plopped the tire to the ground and couldn't help but start laughing myself. I have no idea what the truckers whizzing by must have thought, but I didn't care. God and I were sharing a Hallmark moment, and it was delightful.

We can all have such moments as much as we want if we will just make the connection and keep up the relationship. God is there all the time, and he is waiting for you to make the move, but he will not invade your space. He has come down from heaven to be with you, and he waits eagerly for you to make the move toward him. When you make this move, you will enter a continuing, permanent relationship. Not even death will end it. You establish it here and now, but it transcends death and remains intact throughout all eternity. The apostle Paul tells us that God gives us his Holy Spirit to live in our lives as a sort of down payment, or guarantee, of what he will give us more fully in the future. "You heard and believed the message of truth, the good news that he has saved you. In him you were sealed with the Holy Spirit whom he promised. This Holy Spirit is the guarantee that we will receive our inheritance. We have this guarantee until we are set free to belong to him. God receives praise and glory for this" (Ephesians 1:13–14).

Becoming Transformed

Our confidence in any guarantee depends on our confidence in the party offering it. And that's where we encounter a problem that's pervasive with young people in the church today. Sixty-eight percent of them don't believe the Holy Spirit is a real person.[1] And eighty-one percent believe it is up to them to create their own truth rather than to discover God and his truth in the pages of Scripture.[2] With such distorted views of God's Spirit and the Bible, our young people are robbed of the means God gave us to know that the Holy Spirit is a real person. If Christ and his claims and the presence of the Holy Spirit are true for you only because you choose to believe them, then the Holy Spirit can give you nothing more than the kind of comfort a child finds in an imaginary friend. If you see the Holy Spirit Christ promised as true for you only because you choose to believe it but not objectively true as absolute reality, the guarantee of the Holy Spirit means nothing. Because Christ is who he claimed to be, however, his offer of reconnection to God through the Holy Spirit is real. It can really happen, and it can truly change your life.

One of our crucial tasks as adults is to see that our young people grasp the utter reality of Christ and his Holy Spirit so they can plunge into commitment with assurance that all God's promises are true. These promises are objective reality. Objective reality is what is always there, standing true and solid, even when no one chooses to believe it.

When we speak of the Holy Spirit living in our lives, we want to be clear that we mean what we say. Often the word *spirit* is used to mean an aura or a pervasive atmosphere or a common feeling, as in "the spirit of Christmas" or "school spirit." It is used to mean an emotional bond with others of like mind as when one says, "I couldn't be there in person, but I was there in spirit."

When we say that God's Holy Spirit lives in us, we are not using the term in these senses. The Holy Spirit is not merely an idea or a feeling. He literally exists as an actual living being with intelligence, presence, mind, emotion, and will. When we say that he lives in you, we are not speaking metaphorically. We are not saying that you take on the aura of God or a mindset like God's or a good feeling as if you had the presence of God. We are not saying that if you learn God's will through the Bible it's the same *as if* he were living in you because you have his message in your head. We are using the language as literally, directly, and non-metaphorically as it can be taken. We are saying that the real being who exists as the living God in Spirit form actually places himself literally in your being. God himself becomes your intimate companion. The actual God who created the universe and all things in it establishes a personal relationship with you just as he had with Adam, Abraham, and Moses. He is as good as his promise. He is with us always.

When our young people fail to take into account the vital significance of the Holy Spirit in the life of the Christian, it leads them into a common misconception that the idea of religion is to make people good. They think that in becoming Christians we embark on a program of self-improvement. Through study, diligence, discipline, and sheer effort, we attempt to model our lives after Christ's and thereby become better people. This mistaken way of thinking often takes three common forms.

The first is the idea that we must *perform*. We think we must do something to earn God's love. We think we must work hard and live up to a list of expectations of goodness and diligence. This way of thinking causes us to define ourselves by what we do. We consider ourselves as good or as bad as our behavior and accomplishments. We become convinced that God will love us only if we do enough to please him. This erroneous view is what sixty-four percent of our young people believe.

The second mistaken idea about the Christian life is that we must *conform*—to think we must become like other people in the church to earn their approval as well as God's. We see the principle of conformity all around us in secular society. People earn acceptance by conforming to clothing styles, associating with the right people, living in the right neighborhood, driving the right car, eating at the right restaurants, using the right catchwords and phrases in their speech. Picking up on these cues, some try to earn God's approval by conforming to the expectations of other Christians—joining the right churches, adopting the right beliefs, going through the right rituals. They look around and use others as the model for what a Christian ought to look like, and then they adopt the same look.

The third mistaken conception of the Christian life is that Christians must *reform*. They assume that they must improve their inner nature in order to earn approval. They must overcome that sin nature that wants to be selfish, rude, indulgent, and prideful, and so they subject it to a makeover. They try to discipline themselves to be nice, to overcome bad habits, to obey the rules, to improve their disposition, stifle their temper, replace bad habits, and acquire culture. They think if they reshape their inner nature into one pleasing to God, then he will love and accept them.

All three of these *forms*—perform, conform, and reform—take enormous will power. All are human efforts depending solely on the power of self. God is not involved. We have no one to thank but ourselves for what progress we make. But none of these *forms* produces any real change in our natures. Anything you do by your own effort is like putting makeup on a corpse. It has no effect on the hard reality. Whether we perform, conform, or reform, we are like a burned out light bulb polished up and hoping to impress. But we still produce no light, and God is not impressed.

Our problem is that we can't be merely improved into being what God intends us to be. Remaking ourselves into an image that resembles what God intends misses the whole point of our existence. God in our lives fulfills our purpose for being and is the only source of life for us.

When Adam and Eve rejected God, they cut themselves off from their source of life. They were walking dead people. Like dead batteries or burned out light bulbs, they were useless, meaningless, and unimprovable. No amount of polishing them up or painting or cleaning would change anything. They were dead. We inherit their nature. We are the children of their choice, born into a race that has kicked God out. Until that relationship is reestablished with God and his life is imparted into ours, performing, conforming, or reforming won't solve the basic problem. We are still walking dead people.

Several years ago Twentieth Century Fox released the silly comedy, *Weekend at Bernie's*. Bernie had been rubbed out by the mob, and a couple of young men had to manipulate his corpse to fool people into thinking he was alive. But in spite of the fact that Bernie's body was put through the motions of being alive, he remained dead. Even when a walking dead person imitates life, he or she is still dead. It's the same with Christians. Even when people imitate all the motions of being a Christian, without the Spirit of God in their lives, they are dead.

The only solution is to be *transformed*—not from bad to good or good to better, but from death to life. Christ didn't come to make bad people good or good people better; he came to make dead people live. He came to give us life by placing God's Holy Spirit within us to reestablish the intimate, continuing relationship lost in Eden. This is the sole purpose of religion—"re-ligamenting" us to God. In fact, this connecting with God in relationship is not merely religion, it is the center of reality for every human on earth. Whether to reconnect with God is the single most important choice any person will ever make.

This transformation will indeed mean change. God in your life means utter renovation. He will indeed remake you into a better person if you allow it, but it's by his power spreading into all areas of your life and activating your talents. With God in your life, the light is turned on inside, not polished up on the outside of the bulb.

God has taken extraordinary steps in order for you and me to have an intimate relationship with him. And he will take what you give him, using it as a foothold in your heart to expand his life until it fills your entire being. He is there to give you peace, joy, happiness, and love, so that you can delight in him as he delights in you.

CHAPTER 15

Modeling Continuing Relationships

The pressures of modern marketing mean that publishers today must give bookstores and chains specific publication dates and stick to them. This leads publishers to put immense pressure on writers to complete manuscripts in time to meet printing schedules. I had such a deadline fast approaching that simply couldn't be missed. I was right in the middle of editing a difficult chapter, deep in the throes of heavy concentration, when my then two-year-old son Sean bounced through the door.

"Want to play, Daddy?" he said, holding his new ball in both hands as those big round eyes gazed at me expectantly.

Probably somewhere in the back of my mind I knew that all Sean needed at the moment was a few minutes of my time to toss the ball back and forth or perhaps just to sit for two or three minutes in my lap and marvel over his new ball. But none of these thoughts pushed themselves up through my concern for my deadline. "I can't do it right now, Son. I'm right in the middle of a chapter," I replied. "How about a little later?"

Little Sean didn't know what a chapter was, but he got the message. Daddy was too busy, and he'd have to leave now. He trotted off without complaining, and I returned to my manuscript. But my relief didn't last. A few minutes later, Dottie came in and sat down for one of her gentle "little chats."

"Honey, Sean just told me you were too busy to play with him," she began. "I know how important this book deadline is, but I'd like to point out something."

"What's that?" I asked, a little impatiently, not even looking up from my all-important manuscript.

"I think you need to realize that you will always have writing to do, and you will always have deadlines. Your whole life will be filled with researching and projects, but you're not always going to have a two-year-old son who wants to sit on your lap and show you his new ball."

"I hear what you're saying," I said (though I didn't really), "and you make a lot of sense, as usual. But right now, I've just got to finish this chapter."

"All right, Josh," she replied. "But please think about it. You know, if we spend time with our kids now, they will spend time with us later."

Dottie's good sense did penetrate my concentration, and the more I thought, the more her gentle but perceptive words reached the center of my mind. She was right. Deadlines, contracts, phone calls, meetings, trips—these things would be with me always. But my children would be children only for a moment. The years would sweep by, and I would miss out on the joy of participating in their growing up. And they would miss out on the security of having a real father.

Without any big speeches or fanfare, I made a decision right then and there. I went out of my office, found Sean, and spent a quarter hour playing catch with him. From that moment on, I always tried to place my children ahead of my career, making them my number one priority. It was not always easy, especially not at first. Most of us inadvertently get caught in the time trap before we realize it is happening. We not only have our own work and duties, but we are continually bombarded with needs for volunteer help from civic causes, fund drives, schools, hospitals, and even our churches. These causes are always good and the needs are real, and so a sense of duty or guilt often spurs us to join up and help. In time, we suddenly find the clock and the calendar glutted with good things that need to be done.

But as the British evangelist/theologian Major Ian Thomas has said, "The need is not the call." We must continually remind ourselves of our real priorities and learn to pronounce that short but difficult little two-letter word, "No."

At all costs, we must protect the time necessary to keep our relationship with our kids intact and vital. We must show by our priorities that no person, activity, job, project, or possession is more important than our families.

Why is it so important that adults become involved in the lives of children? One answer is obvious: they need adult supervision, correction, and role modeling as they grow into maturity. But there's more. The reason that our young people don't move toward an intimate relationship with God is that they are not thoroughly convinced in their own hearts that he is the one true God. As we have seen in the statistics we quoted earlier, most of them are not convinced that he is historically real or that he rose from the dead and gave his Spirit to live intimately in their hearts today. Our task, therefore, is to show them the heart of God who longs for a relationship with them and lead them to understand the reality of who he is so that they can enter that relationship with confidence. And we show this relationship by modeling relationship.

When committed Christians establish meaningful relationships with young persons, they demonstrate to them the love of God and also expose them to it. We bring God into the life of our young people by making our continued presence a positive force in shaping their lives. Being available to the kids in your environment says to them exactly what God's availability says to you: "You are important. I love you enough not just to provide the necessities for you, but also to be with you, and to enjoy a relationship with you."

Even Christ thought it was important to give time to children. When some parents brought their children to Jesus so he could bless them, his disciples thought the little urchins swarming about the Master was a bother and unworthy of his attention. They tried to shoo the kids away, but Jesus said, "Don't stop children from coming to me! Children like these are part of the kingdom of God" (Matthew 19:14). If Jesus, who came to save the world and continually endured the clamor of people with desperate needs thought it important to spend time with children, how much more should we?

The tragedy that can come when we don't spend time with our kids is vividly illustrated by the heartbreaking story of a woman who approached me after hearing me speak at a local church on this very subject. Tears filled her eyes as she explained that she was the wife of a senior vice president of a huge corporation. "My husband just died," she said. "He was a multimillion-dollar-a-year man. He traveled all over the world constructing major projects, but he never took time for his children, even when he was home. All of them turned against him, and when they were grown, they would have nothing to do with him. On his deathbed, he confessed to me that he was dying as one of the saddest men in the world. He told me, 'I gained prestige, but I lost my family. I gained wealth, but I lost my children. If only I had spent more time with them.'"

As she sadly told her story, I remembered Dottie's wise comment when Sean wanted to play ball with me: "If we spend time with our kids now, they will spend time with us later."

Kids Spell Love T-I-M-E

It has become trite to say that today we live in a hectic, fast-paced society, so we won't say it. But you know it is true. Couples today work one thousand hours more each year than they did thirty years ago. People just can't find the time to squeeze in everything they need to do, much less everything they want to do. The easy way out is to focus on what must be done just to keep things running and postpone or abandon activities not tied to immediate demands.

More often than not, it's family time that gets cut. It may shock you to know just how little time most parents spend with their kids. A study I commissioned a few years ago shows that sixty-six percent of churched youth spend an average of less than four and one-half minutes per day with their fathers, and sixty-two percent spend an average of a little more than eight and one-half minutes per day with their mothers.[1] Those dismal statistics compare to a minimum of four hours per day teens spend with various forms of mass media.[2] It will be hard to convince our kids that they are important to us when we let the media take up twenty-six to forty-eight times more of their lives than we do. It's true that time is hard to find these days. It has become one of our most valuable commodities, and one that we try desperately to hoard and protect. But if we want our kids to know that they are loved and cherished, there is no substitute for sacrificing more of our time for them.

No doubt you have heard people say, "I can't spend nearly as much time with Jenny as I'd like, but I make sure that what time I do give her is quality time." By "quality time" parents usually mean scheduled special events such as a trip to an amusement park or an afternoon at the beach. These sporadic big events dropped into a desert of inattention do not make up for lack of time any more than an occasional night at an all-you-can-eat buffet makes up for a week of starvation. Of course, we all want quality time with our kids, but we don't necessarily get the quality by putting it on a schedule. The intimacy needed to produce quality will not be there at the scheduled time if it has not been regularly maintained with ongoing involvement in their lives. Quality can't happen without intimacy, which must be developed continually over time. And quality time is often unpredictable. Quality moments come unexpectedly. They are serendipities, and you can't know when they might spring forth.

Our (Tom's) family often enjoyed more spontaneous banter and laughter sitting around the table after dinner than when I took them to a comedy at the movie theater. My daughter learned more about the "birds and the bees" when we witnessed the unexpected event of our dog having puppies than she would from a scheduled session with my wife and a medical manual.

To get the benefit of the unexpected moments and build a meaningful, continuing relationship, you've got to be there. It's the ongoing involvement in the everyday little moments that add up to a loving relationship. When parents are not involved in their kids' lives on a day-to-day basis, children will have trouble thinking the parents really love them deeply. But when it becomes obvious to your kids that you are giving up needs or even preferences to be with them or do things for them, they will come to realize that they are important to you.

Carpe Diem!

Of course we've got to be realistic. You must work, not only to earn a living but also to keep the household running. You can't literally be with your kids all the time or even most of the time. But you can make them integral and continuing parts of your lives. Most of us can find more time, and we can learn to use what time we have to good advantage. We can include them in as much of our lives as possible and develop a relational mindset when we are with them. We can impart to them a positive, Christian worldview by our conversation, by the activities we involve them in, and by the acts they witness us performing. It's not all that hard. A passage in Deuteronomy gives us the key. Speaking of the words God had taught to the Israelites at Sinai, it says: "Teach them to your children, and talk about them when you are at home or away, when you lie down or get up" (Deuteronomy 11:19). In other words, make your children an important and regular part of your life, and be continually alert for ways to mold and teach them.

As the popular Latin phrase says, *Carpe Diem!* Seize the day! Develop a continuing attitude that alerts you to seize the moments, involving your kids in the everyday routines of your lives in order to deepen the relationship. Take one or more of them with you as you run errands or make short trips, and talk with them as you travel. Work with them on their projects and invite them to work with you on yours. Let them help you when you're planting flowers, building a patio deck, baking a pie, or painting the fence. Make it a priority to have as many evening meals together as possible. Keep these times upbeat and free of chastisement, criticism, or controversy. Be with your kids in their successes and failures, celebrate their important moments, and include them in your own important moments. I know one father who takes his four-year-old son with him to the podium when he does Bible readings or prayers in his church. I watched one young mother in Wal-Mart explaining to her young daughter how to compare prices and weights on food packages. I knew a minister who always took a teenager from his church with him when he went on weekend mission trips. In short, make your young people an integral part of your life and become an integral part of theirs. They need more than just the big special events; they need an ongoing relationship—the kind of ongoing relationship that God has with us. Such relationships with you will lead them to want to know your God.

Adults involved with kids, whether they are parents, grandparents, youth workers, or teachers, cannot maintain a distance from them most of the time then suddenly expect a strong bond to connect them when they eventually find a moment to do something together. Relationship is a process. It cannot be sporadic; to be authentic and meaningful, it must be continual—nurtured and maintained on an ongoing basis.

The Teen Years

Some parents make the mistake of thinking the formative years are over when their children enter adolescence. As teens become more independent in their activities, schedules, and thought, parents often allow a gap to grow between them and their children. But the formative years are far from over when the height soars, the voice deepens, or the figure begins to round out. They still need—and secretly want—strong connections with adults. And it's up to the adults to make it happen. In spite of busy and conflicting schedules, parents can insist on family time together, especially at evening meals and on weekends. Parents must make the effort to stay involved in their kids' lives, showing interest in their activities, complimenting them on their successes, and giving them loving understanding and acceptance in their failures.

Probe their thinking; get their take on current issues and questions about morality and Christianity. Learn the art of asking questions so you can seize the moments you have with your kids. Go beyond merely asking the perfunctory, "So how was your day?" Take the plunge and ask more probing questions such as:

- What have you always wanted to do that we've never done together as a family (or youth group)?

- If you could change our family (or youth group), how would you change it?

- If you were the father or mother (or youth leader), what would you do differently?

- What makes you happy? What makes you sad?

- If you could ask God one question, what would it be?

- If you had a million dollars, how would you spend it?

- If you were God for a day, what would you do?

- If you could visit any place in the world, where would you go?

When you ask such questions, brace yourself for frank answers and be ready to discuss these answers amicably without criticism or condemnation. Remember that your purpose in asking these questions is to initiate openness and discussion, and a frank answer means you are succeeding. Be happy about it; it shows that the young person is being open with you. Treat their opinions with respect and correct their thinking when necessary with understanding and gentleness. The more they sense that you are truly interested in what they think and feel, the more they will understand how dearly they are cherished, and the more intimate the relationship will become.

Passing On God's Love

By being continually available to our young people, we model the love and closeness of Christ who promised shortly before he ascended into heaven, "I am always with you" (Matthew 28:20). He continually fulfills that promise to those who enter a relationship with him. He is with us always, even as near as our next breath. The presence of the Holy Spirit in our lives is loving, intimate, and continual. He is always there for us.

When we make ourselves available to our kids in a continual, loving relationship, we show that, like God, we are always there for them. We become role models showing them the nature of God, introducing them to his love, and drawing them into a relationship that includes God at the fountainhead. We show them that we have nothing that God did not give us, including love.

When he enters a permanent, continual relationship with us, he pours his love into us continually so that we become overflowing cups, pouring out his love to others. We are like lakes with a stream of love flowing in and filling us and then flowing outward in a continual stream to others. Because God's love is continual, we are never empty, no matter how much of his love we pass along in our ongoing relationships. In loving others, especially our youth, we fulfill the role for which we were created and become conduits for the love of God. That is the essence of what it means to live the Christian life.

When kids are in godly relationships, their obedience is not compelled under the duress of imposed rules; instead they obey willingly, motivated by the interplay of love. They become increasingly more like the person to whom they relate. Therefore, if we relate to Christ and allow his life to transform ours, our kids will be transformed more into his likeness by their relationship to us.

You will see two happy results in the lives of young people who catch the Christlike modeling you give them. First, they will be much more likely to make better choices between right and wrong. Making right choices is connected to relationship because when they accept God's invitation to intimate companionship with him, he will give them his Holy Spirit to empower them to make right choices. This both honors God and brings them blessing.

Second, your Christlike modeling motivates your young people into a spiritual formation process. They will want to become more like Christ, and as that transformation occurs, they will, in turn, become models themselves. They will be led to love others with the same love that he gives them. We are not suggesting that they will immediately morph into perfect little angels. Learning to love others and to make godly choices is a process. No one learns it once and for all in a study course; we learn it throughout the course of life. And the key is to understand that right relationships and right choices are directly related to our love relationship with God.

Bonus Section

How We Know The Bible Is Reliable

Preface to the Bonus Section

This bonus section is provided to help you go deeper into the reasons for why we can trust the Bible. You will notice that this last section is written differently than what you have been reading. It is written in more of a reference text style. As such, it will become an easy reference guide when your family has questions about the reliability of Scripture. For even more in-depth study and reference, I encourage you to obtain a copy of *The New Evidence That Demands a Verdict*.

An explanation of that book is found on page 248.

Both this section and *New Evidence* are tools to help you teach the young people in your life to know why they believe what they believe. The claims Christ made about himself and his Word are fully reliable, dependable, and real. I pray that you will find this section and the other resources we have created for you useful and effective.

— Josh McDowell

CHAPTER 1

Why We Must Have a Reliable Bible

Now that we have led you through the steps of God's progressive revelation—from the Bible, to the person of Jesus Christ, to the Holy Spirit living in us, to our charge to reveal God to others—we find that the steps lead us full circle back to our starting place. One might easily conclude that since God's revelation is progressive, growing more intimate with each step, that by the end of the process the Bible becomes expendable. Once we have absorbed the Bible's living and dynamic revelations of God in Jesus and the Holy Spirit and moved into relationship with him, can't we just discard the book and live by the intimate power of the Holy Spirit? No, that would be disastrous. When we use the term "progressive revelation," the progression is not like that of an automobile trip whereby you leave each town behind as you move on down the road to the next. Rather it is like the progression of an automobile assembly line where at each station a new part is added until at the end the car is complete. When you meet Christ and add the Holy Spirit to your life, you don't discard the Bible as you might discard the instructions after you assemble your barbecue grill. The Bible is of critical value to us. Let's briefly explore why.

The Bible Introduces Us to the Truth of Christ

We have emphasized in this book that the essence of Christianity is not its rules for behavior or as a road map to heaven. It is a person. Without the person of Christ, dying for our sins and giving us his Holy Spirit to live in us, Christianity would be meaningless and superfluous. It would be just another religion with nothing to lift it above the false religions that compete with it. But since the basis and authenticity of Christianity rest on a person, it is imperative that we know for sure that that person existed, what he said and what he did, and that he was exactly who he said he was.

If Christ is not who he claims to be, then Christianity is useless. It is merely another myth designed to explain incomprehensible reality or to provide a temporary illusion of comfort to keep us from despairing at the tragic futility of existence.

The culture conditions young people to think that mere belief is enough to validate one's truth. Choose your version of truth, believe in it strongly enough, and it will work for you, and no one else should question what you have chosen to believe. But this approach simply won't work. Ultimately, anyone who holds to any personal belief that is not grounded in absolute truth will come away empty. No mere belief, no matter how sincerely held, can meet our human desires or solve our relational needs. Just as a phone call is futile unless there is someone on the other end of the line, a belief is futile unless there is a reality out there to validate it. When our belief reaches out, it much touch a hand reaching back. To do us any good, Christianity must be more than the product of wishful thinking disguised as faith. It must be true objectively. The only Christ who can meet our needs is a Christ who is real—a Christ with whom we can make a solid connection and establish a relationship.

Our source for reliable information about Christ is the Bible. Without the Bible, we would not have a clear revelation of him; we would not know how to conform our lives to his; we would not know of his perfect life, his sacrifice, or his call for us to become one with him. The Bible is essential to our knowledge of who Jesus Christ is, what he did for us, and how to establish a relationship with him through the Holy Spirit.

How Do We Know the Bible Is True?

If we look to the Bible as our revelation of Christ, another question must be answered if we are to be assured that what we believe is true. How do we know the Bible is reliable? That's the question behind the question. How do we know who Christ is? The Bible tells us. But how do we know we can trust the Bible? The answer to that question is essential to our confidence of the absolute truth of what we believe and teach our young people about Christ and Christianity. That is why I have chosen to append this book about the relational nature of the Word with solid evidence that will help you convince them of the reliability of the Scriptures.

Knowing God, living in relationship with him, and reflecting his likeness in every facet of our lives are all dependent upon our receiving and possessing an accurate revelation of him. Without a reliable Bible to use as a guide and a mirror, we have no assurance that we can conform our lives to the likeness of Christ. While the Holy Spirit is certainly there to empower us to live like Christ, how can we be sure we correctly understand his leadings? The Scriptures are given so that we can "test the spirits" to see if we are being led in God's direction. If we didn't have an accurate and reliable Bible to test our direction, we would be left to fumble in the dark, following our own thinking and being led by our own feelings, never knowing for sure that we had found real truth.

Peter understood that there was no real alternative to finding true life than in Christ himself. He said, "Lord to what person could we go? Your words give eternal life" (John 6:68). But what if the things Jesus said—the words of eternal life—were changed or exaggerated down through the years? If the words God gave to Moses, David, Matthew, and Peter were later changed or carelessly copied, how could we be sure we are coming to know the one true God? How could we be confident that the commands we're obeying are a true reflection of God's nature and character? If we hope to enjoy the relational benefits of knowing God, we must have assurance that our Bible accurately represents what God inspired people to write on his behalf. Because if we don't— if God's message was not accurately recorded and relayed to us—

then we and our children have no objective standard by which to know what God and his Son are truly like.

There is, however, overwhelming evidence to assure us that what is written in the Bible has been (1) relayed to us accurately (bibliographic evidence), (2) recorded exactly (internal evidence), and (3) reinforced externally (external evidence). Details of each of these assuring evidences are documented at length in this section.

In the following chapters, I will draw on information I uncovered in my own extensive search for the truth about the Bible to demonstrate why we can know for sure that the Bible is true, the incarnation really happened, and Christ is everything he claimed to be.[1] These truths are not just unauthenticated claims. The facts of the incarnation are verifiable historical realities. Jesus did not merely say, "I love you too much to abandon you to your fate." He came in real time to a given geographical location on this planet to show that he meant it. And the deed was not done in secret or hidden from observation but was viewed and recorded by eyewitnesses. In fact, the Bible is overwhelmingly the best documented and most thoroughly authenticated of all ancient writings in existence. We will explore this evidence in the following chapters to give our young people confidence in the truth of Christianity's claims.

CHAPTER 2

The Bible Is Reliable:
Internal Evidence

F ew Christians make it far into life without encountering challenges to the truth and reliability of the Bible. It may have been hushed whispers contradicting a Sunday school teacher or a high school coach or boss or some other adult in a position of authority ridiculing the gullibility of anyone naïve enough to believe the Bible. Certainly, every student in a secular university has heard professors unleash a barrage of arguments against a Christian classmate. Most of us, if we are honest enough to admit it, remember how in moments of quietness unbeckoned questions just popped into our own minds about whether or not Scripture was really reliable.

Rather than meeting the challenge straight on, the first impulse of many Christians is to avoid those questions. They feel a wave of guilt and confusion when they entertain even the most fleeting concerns about the Bible's authorship or authority. Unfortunately, some never seek adequate answers, letting their doubts fester and grow until they simply discard their faith. Others become fruitful members of Bible-believing churches, holding tenaciously or even desperately to their faith while still lacking a secure foundation for believing. Their personal beliefs remain firm, but they are not equipped to persuade others to believe the truth.

As much as we might wish that we could shelter our young people from challenges to their faith, they cannot escape them. By the time they're in high school, most Christian youth are deeply entrenched in the postmodern belief that says no truth is absolute (i.e., true for everyone). And it's inevitable that college students will hear that biblical accounts are wild exaggerations or total fabrications.

Such challenges demand credible answers if our young people are to develop deep, solid, and lasting Christian convictions.

As I've already said, our faith would be badly shaken if the Bible were not reliable. That intimate relationship with Christ that we want our young people to experience cannot be real unless he is exactly who the Bible claims him to be. It follows, then, that their faith will be solidly grounded when they have confidence that what the Bible tells us is true. This understanding is critical to a faith that will hold them firm and steady in the midst of an increasingly godless culture. What we are looking for is truth, which is, by definition, a view of the world that is "ideal or fundamental reality apart from and transcending perceived experience."[1] That's what truth is all about. We don't want mere opinions based on subjective experience; we want to deal in reality.

Testing the Facts

Christians hold that the Bible is *inspired*, that is, while humans wrote the words, God himself inspired or directed its content. While that understanding is meaningful to us as believers, it is not an adequate starting point for persuading others that Scripture is reliable. For an objective evaluation of its veracity, we must be willing to subject the Bible to the three tests that can scholars apply to any work of historical literature:

- The *internal evidence* test: Can the book stand up to tests of internal validity?

- The *bibliographic* test: Has the text of the work been transmitted accurately?

- The *external evidence* test: Has the book been reinforced by data outside itself?

We have a mountain of evidence showing that the Bible passes all three of these tests with ease. In this chapter, we will focus on the internal evidence test. I cannot in the few pages allotted here give you the mountain of evidence available to support the Bible's internal reliability, but we will look briefly at a few significant samplings of this evidence.

The Internal Evidence Test

The internal evidence test weighs whether a book is consistent within itself and whether the authors can be trusted to tell the truth. Is the book filled with contradictions? Is there evidence that the bias of the writers overcame their objectivity and distorted the facts? Let's check the Bible's historical credibility by the three standards used to test the internal reliability of all historical documents:

- the benefit of the doubt
- freedom from contradiction
- the use of primary sources.

Internal Reliability Standard 1: Giving the Text the Benefit of the Doubt

All of us can recall instances when we felt treated unfairly by an authority figure—a teacher or boss or parent. The person had prejudged us and decided that no matter what we did it was wrong. We were judged guilty until proven innocent.

Many critics develop that same unfair attitude toward certain books and especially toward the Bible. They come to the book with a prejudice against the possibility of miracles or with a resistance to the Bible's claim to be authoritative. They treat every unexplained detail as an error and find discrepancies where none exist. Readers must approach any book—Scripture included—with objective openness to the statements of the author. Disliking or having difficulty with a doctrine, a fact of history, or a truth claim does not mean it should be regarded as untrue. John Warwick Montgomery, one of today's foremost Christian apologists, stated a principle first established by Aristotle when he said, "One must listen to the claims of the document under analysis, and not assume fraud or error unless the author disqualified himself by contradictions or known factual inaccuracies."[2] Whether evaluating the Bible or any other book, we have an obligation simply to be fair. If the text of a book is "innocent until proven guilty," the burden of proof is on the critic to show that a difficulty within the Bible constitutes a real error.

Internal Reliability Standard 2: Freedom from Known Contradictions

"The Bible can't be trusted because it is full of contradictions." We've all heard the charge, and we've all read passages that seem at first glance to be contradictory. However, an objective reading of such passages usually shows that while some may be difficult to reconcile, reconciliation is not impossible. Also, in passing, it's worth noting that none of these difficulties occur on major doctrines or events in the Bible. They are all relegated to minor details which are insignificant to the overarching message of Scripture and have no bearing on its doctrines. Yet critics will point to the smallest detail that seems contradictory and say, "Aha! If we can't trust the Bible to be accurate in the tiny details, how can we trust its major pronouncements?"

Some staunch Christians whose faith and reason are unassailable are willing to accept the possibility of minor discrepancies. Some, for example, find the apparent discrepancies in the four gospel accounts concerning the details surrounding the events at the empty tomb on Easter morning to be faith-affirming rather than undermining. If all four accounts were identical, they say, we would suspect collusion between the writers. The differing viewpoints on insignificant details serve only to show by contrast the amazing agreement of the whole on matters of substance.

Yet many evangelical Bible scholars find that what seems to be minor discrepancies are not necessarily actual inconsistencies. To deal objectively with the Bible and evaluate its truthfulness as we would any other book, we need to discern the difference between what constitutes a genuine mistake versus a lack of knowledge on the part of the reader.

In evaluating ancient manuscripts, objective scholars apply a principle that any alleged contradictions in the work must be demonstrated to be impossible to reconcile, not merely difficult. Author Robert M. Horn describes the conditions we must meet to demonstrate that a text contains genuine mistakes. Far more is required, he says, than "the mere appearance of a contradiction." First, we must be certain we have understood a passage properly—how it uses words and numbers, for example. Second, we must know all that can be reasonably known about the subject treated in the text. And third, we must be sure that new discoveries in textual research, archaeology, and so on couldn't possibly shed more light on the passage. Horn concludes: "Difficulties do not constitute objections. Unsolved problems are not of necessity errors. This is not to minimize the area of difficulty; it is to see it in perspective. Difficulties are to be grappled with and problems are to drive us to seek clearer light; but until such time as we have total and final light on any issue we are in no position to affirm, 'Here is a proven error, an unquestionable objection to an infallible Bible.'"[3] Horn reinforces the importance of this test when he notes that countless supposed errors in the Bible have been fully answered in the past century.

For example, critics once insisted that Moses could not have written the first five books of the Bible because writing did not exist in Moses' day. However, subsequent archaeology has shown that writing existed at least two thousand years before Moses. Critics once said the Bible was erroneous in its mention of the Hittites, a people who appeared in no other historical documents, yet historians now know the Hittites existed because an ancient Hittite library has been found in Turkey. These and many other charges against the Bible have yielded to the rapidly increasing knowledge of history, archaeology, linguistics, and other disciplines.

Such allegations of error in the Bible often flow from a failure to observe the basic principles of interpreting ancient literature. Following is a list of the ten major interpretive principles that help scholars discern whether there is a clear error or a contradiction in any literature—in this case, the Bible:

Principle 1: The unexplained is not necessarily unexplainable.

Scientists once had no natural explanation of meteors, eclipses, tornadoes, hurricanes, or earthquakes, but scientists did not throw in the towel and say that all of science was hogwash. Christian scholars likewise approach the Bible with the same presumption that what is currently *unexplained* isn't therefore *unexplainable*. They simply continue to do research. It is a mistake to assume that what has not yet been explained will *never* be explained.

Principle 2: Conflicts between the Bible and scientific theory don't prove the Bible false.

Many prevailing views of science in the past are considered errors by scientists in the present. In addition, many concepts presented to us as scientific fact are actually merely unproven theories. We can't assume that today's scientific theories are the final word on reality. The changing state of knowledge means that popular opinions in science will often clash with widely accepted interpretations of the Bible. Conflict between Scripture and changing theories of science does not prove the Bible false.

Principle 3: The context of the passage controls the meaning.

You can prove anything from the Bible if you take words out of context. The Bible says, "There is no God" (Psalm 14:1, NIV). The context, of course, is that "The fool has said in his heart, 'There is no God.'" Likewise, some fail to understand the context of Jesus' statement "Give to him who asks you." Does this mean that one should give a gun to a small child who asks—or nuclear weapons to a terrorist because he asks? Failure to consider passages in their context is one of the major errors of Bible critics.

Principle 4: Clear passages illuminate cloudy ones.

Some Bible passages appear to contradict others. John 3:16 speaks of loving the world while the same author in 1 John 2:15 says to "stop loving this evil world." But as we read on in 1 John, we find the clear explanation: he speaks of shunning the evil temptations the world offers, whereas in John 3:16 the clear meaning is loving the people of the world. To jump on these passages as contradictory is to abandon the common sense we use in interpreting everyday language.

Principle 5: The Bible is a book for humans with human characteristics.

Countless college professors point to Psalm 19:6 as an obvious case of the Bible's fallibility: "The sun rises at one end of the heavens and follows its course to the other end" (NLT). We've known for centuries that the sun does not move around the earth; the earth's rotation merely causes the sun to appear to move. The same professor can speak in the next breath of watching a beautiful "sunset," ignoring the fact that a term can be nonscientific without being inaccurate. The Bible uses nontechnical, everyday expressions of speech and well-known literary devices. It uses round numbers in some places and exact numbers in others. None of these instances of normal use of language amount to contradictions.

Principle 6: An incomplete report is not a false report.

Mark 5:1–20 and Luke 8:26–39 speak of Jesus encountering a demoniac in Gadara while the parallel account in Matthew 8:28–34 tells us there were two demoniacs. Is this a contradiction? Mark and Luke, neither of whom were eyewitnesses to the event, could have recorded a report that focused on the more prominent of two demoniacs and ignored the other. Their accounts may be less complete, but they are not contradictory. Matthew simply supplies more information.

Principle 7: The Bible doesn't endorse all it records.

Many readers wonder whether the Bible promotes polygamy when it tallies up Solomon's many wives (1 Kings 11:3) or if it affirms cheating in Jacob's successful stealing of his brother's birthright. It's a mistake, however, to think that everything reported in the Bible is commended by the Bible. The Bible records lies, immorality, dishonesty, and faithlessness not to condone but to relate events truthfully.

Principle 8: Errors in copies do not equate to errors in the originals.
When scholars speak of the "inerrancy" of the Scriptures, they
are referring to the Bible as originally written—the first manuscripts or "autographs"—as opposed to a copy or a copy of a
copy. Scholars can compare large numbers of early Bible manuscripts to weed out obvious copying errors, thus determining the
original text with great certainty.

***Principle 9: General statements are not necessarily universal
promises.***
Critics often seize upon Bible verses that offer general truths and
point to obvious exceptions. Some biblical statements are obvious
generalizations. Proverbs 16:7 says that "when a person's ways
are pleasing to the Lord, he makes even his enemies to be at
peace with him." This statement obviously wasn't meant as a
universal promise. Paul pleased the Lord, but his enemies stoned
him (Acts 14:19). Jesus pleased the Lord, yet his enemies crucified him. It is a valid general principle that acting in a way pleasing to God often attracts others—even enemies.

Principle 10: Later revelation supercedes previous revelation.
Under the Mosaic Law, God commanded that animals be sacrificed for people's sin. Since Christ offered the perfect sacrifice for
sin (Hebrews 10:11–14), this Old Testament command is no
longer in force. The change isn't a contradiction but an example
of progressive revelation. Later revelation sometimes replaces
former. Bible critics, though, sometimes interpret such changes of
revelation as mistakes.

When the supposed errors in the Bible are subjected to these
tests used in the study of all history and literature, its credibility
survives undamaged. In the foreword to his *Encyclopedia of Bible
Difficulties*, Gleason Archer, former chairman of the department
of Old Testament at Trinity Evangelical Divinity School, gives this
testimony about the internal consistency of the Bible.

> As I have dealt with one apparent discrepancy after
> another and have studied the alleged contradictions

between the biblical record and the evidence of linguistics, archaeology, or science, my confidence in the trustworthiness of Scripture has been repeatedly verified and strengthened by the discovery that almost every problem in Scripture that has ever been discovered by man, from ancient times until now, has been dealt with in a completely satisfactory manner by the biblical text itself—or else by objective archaeological information. [4]

The Bible readily meets the second test of internal reliability, being free from known contradiction. We can approach the Bible with confidence, untroubled by apparent difficulties. We have reason to agree with Mark Twain when he said that it was not the part of the Bible he did not understand that bothered him the most, but the parts he did understand! [5]

Internal Reliability Test 3: The Use of Primary Sources

In 2003, Jason Blair, a reporter for the *New York Times*, was fired for using invented sources, fabricating information, and plagiarizing material used in the nearly seven hundred stories he filed while at the *Times*. Credible newspapers insist on primary sources to authenticate all stories, and furthermore, they want those sources identified and determined to be reliable.[6]

A survey of ancient writings shows that many writers adhered only loosely to the facts of the events they reported. Some highly regarded authors of the ancient world, for example, bear an eerie resemblance to Blair, reporting events that took place many years before they were born and in countries they had never visited. While their writing may be largely factual, historians admit that greater credibility must be granted to writers who were both geographically and chronologically close to the events they reported.

In vivid contrast, the overwhelming weight of scholarship confirms that the accounts of Jesus' life, the history of the early church, and the letters that form the bulk of the New Testament were all written by men who were either eyewitnesses to the events they recorded or contemporaries of eyewitnesses. These "primary sources" lend solid reliability to the text of Scripture.

Gospel writers Matthew, Mark, and John could say such things as, "This report is from an eyewitness giving an accurate account" (John 19:35, NLT). Luke the physician, who wrote the third gospel and the book of Acts, used as source material "the reports circulating among us from the early disciples and other eyewitnesses of what God has done in fulfillment of his promises." He used these accurate testimonies in order to "reassure you of the truth of all you were taught" (Luke 1:2, NLT). Matthew and John were eyewitnesses themselves, enabling John to say, "We are telling you about what we ourselves have actually seen and heard" (1 John 1:3, NLT). The apostle Peter also was an eyewitness, as he affirmed in his second letter, "For we did not follow cunningly devised fables when we made known to you the power and coming of our Lord Jesus Christ, but were eyewitnesses of His majesty" (2 Peter 1:16, NKJV). The apostle Paul, the most prolific New Testament writer, was an eyewitness to Jesus on the Damascus road and mixed regularly with other apostles and witnesses to the life of Jesus on earth.

Some suppose it would be easy for these early disciples to fabricate stories about Jesus. But F. F. Bruce, the former Rylands Professor of Biblical Criticism and Exegesis at the University of Manchester, disputes this allegation. Concerning the value of the eyewitness accounts of the New Testament records, he says:

> The earliest preachers of the gospel knew the value of . . . first-hand testimony, and appealed to it time and again. "We are witnesses of these things," was their constant and confident assertion. And it can have been by no means so easy as some writers seem to think to invent words and deeds of Jesus in those early years, when so many of His disciples were about, who could remember what had and had not happened.[7]

These eyewitnesses are all the more credible because they appealed to the knowledge of their readers—even their most severe opponents—who could easily have contradicted any false accounts. Yet these authors of Scripture invited correction by eyewitnesses to their claims when they said such things as the following:

- "People of Israel, listen! God publicly endorsed Jesus of Nazareth by doing wonderful miracles, wonders, and signs through him, as *you well know*" (Acts 2:22, NLT, italics added).

- "At this point Festus interrupted Paul's defense. 'You are out of your mind, Paul!' he shouted. 'Your great learning is driving you insane.' 'I am not insane, most excellent Festus,' Paul replied. 'What I am saying is true and reasonable. The king is familiar with these things, and I can speak freely to him. I am convinced that *none of this has escaped his notice, because it was not done in a corner*'" (Acts 26:24–26, NIV, italics added).

We find similar appeals in Acts 2:32, 3:15, and 13:31, as well as 1 Corinthians 15:3–8. Bruce points out, ". . . One of the strong points in the original apostolic preaching is the confident appeal to the knowledge of the hearers; they not only said, 'We are witnesses of these things,' but also, 'As you yourselves also know' (Acts 2:22). Had there been any tendency to depart from the facts in any material respect, the possible presence of hostile witnesses in the audience would have served as a further corrective."[8]

The disciples were saying in effect, "Check it out," "Ask around," "You know this as well as I do!" Such challenges demonstrate a supreme confidence that what they recorded was absolutely factual. Bruce summarizes, "And it was not only friendly eyewitnesses that the early preachers had to reckon with; there were others less well disposed who were also conversant with the main facts of the ministry and death of Jesus. The disciples could not afford to risk inaccuracies (not to speak of willful manipulation of the facts), which would at once be exposed by those who would be only too glad to do so."[9] The disciples spoke directly to those who violently opposed them, saying, in effect, "You too know these facts are true. I dare you to disprove me!" That's a foolish approach if you are spreading lies.

The Authenticity of the New Testament Accounts

Some might object to this strand of evidence, saying, "Come on, Josh, that's only what the writers claimed. A pseudo-author writing a century or more after the fact can claim anything." What if this objection was true—that the accounts recorded in the Gospels were contrivances of authors much later than the disciples. Such writers could easily have concocted not only the miracles of Christ and his resurrection, but also the challenges by Jesus' disciples for their hearers to check out the truthfulness of their accounts.

The fact is, however, that the books of the New Testament were written during the lifetimes of those involved in the accounts themselves, not a century or more after the events they described. Said William Foxwell Albright, one of the world's foremost biblical archaeologists: "We can already say emphatically that there is no longer any solid basis for dating any book of the New Testament after about a.d. 80, two full generations before the date between 130 and 150 given by the more radical New Testament critics of today."[10] Albright reiterated this point in an interview published a few years later in *Christianity Today*.[11] Albright also found that the discoveries of the Dead Sea Scrolls at Qumran confirmed his dating of the New Testament within the lifetimes of Jesus' disciples—"the New Testament proves to be in fact what it was formerly believed to be: the teaching of Christ and his immediate followers between cir. 25 and cir. 80 a.d."[12]

Montgomery assures us that scholars today must regard the New Testament as a competent primary source document from the first century.[13] Indeed, even many liberal scholars are being forced to consider earlier dates for the New Testament. Anglican bishop and theologian Dr. John A. T. Robinson, who was certainly no conservative, reaches some startling conclusions in his groundbreaking book *Redating the New Testament*. His research convinced him that the whole of the New Testament was written before the fall of Jerusalem in a.d. 70.[13]

Conclusion

Ample evidence exists to show that the men who wrote the Bible for the most part had firsthand knowledge of the events they recorded or had access to people who had witnessed those events. We have no reason to deny that the words of the Bible are true. The text is free of known contradictions and rooted in the accounts of eyewitnesses. The recorded events are historically factual. With the Bible so thoroughly verified in its empirical data, we have every reason to trust the truth of its doctrines and commands. The Bible passes all tests and withstands all challenges to give us the information we need to come to know God and his relational purpose for our lives.

Chapter 3

The Bible Is Reliable:
Bibliographic Evidence

Of all the books composed since the dawn of civilization, no other book has been so widely distributed in so many languages as the Bible. Literally billions of Bibles have been sold. According to the United Bible Society's 2005 Scripture Distribution Report, member organizations of the UBS in that year alone distributed worldwide more than 24 million complete Bibles and another 11.2 million New Testaments. The UBS also reports that the Bible or portions of the Bible have been translated into more than 2,000 languages. These languages represent the primary vehicle of communication for well over ninety percent of the world's population.[1]

The Bible's phenomenal popularity, however, doesn't guarantee its reliability. The untold millions of Bibles we possess today are printed copies based on ancient handwritten copies of yet other copies of the original. None of the originals exist today.

In our electronic age we take for granted the accurate transmission of documents. We compose our words on-screen, saving electronic files to hard drives and backing them up for safekeeping. We can color-code changes within documents, run utilities to detect flaws in copies, and encrypt files to prevent tampering. We can instantaneously multiply documents around the world via the Internet, and when we finally commit a document to print, we can be certain each copy is an exact replica of the original.

The Bible, in contrast, was composed and transmitted in an era many centuries before printing presses. If a document was to be preserved and passed down to the next generation, the manuscript had to be written by hand. Over time, the ink faded and the material it was written on deteriorated, so the document had to be hand copied periodically or it would be lost forever.

To our modern minds, this copying process seems vulnerable to human error and tampering, thus casting doubt on the reliable transmission of Scripture. Who can say that a scribe didn't omit a few words? What if years later someone decided to add new material to the text? How do we know that a weary copier, blurry-eyed from lack of sleep, didn't skip whole sections or mis-quote key verses? In other words, even if the Bible's human authors recorded exactly what God inspired them to write, how can we believe that what we read today is what they originally wrote? How can we be sure that the manuscripts available to us today are an accurate transmission of the originals?

Our brief examination of the internal reliability of the Bible in the previous chapter gave us reason for confidence in its accuracy in the original manuscripts. Now, by examining the Bible's bibli-ographic reliability, we will find certainty that we have received the truth, even through generations of copying. The overwhelm-ing weight of evidence affirms that what was originally recorded has been correctly conveyed through the centuries so that when you pick up a Bible today, you can be utterly confident that you are holding a well-preserved, fully reliable document.

The Reliability of Ancient Writings

Although we don't possess the original manuscripts for the Bible, we can subject copies of it to the same scrutiny we apply to other writ-ings from the ancient world. We can put Scripture to the test using the two standards by which historians evaluate the textual reliabil-ity of ancient literature. These tests concern the number of copies we possess and the relative age of those copies. Historians ask

1. How many manuscript copies are available?

2. What interval of time passed between the original writing and the earliest existing (or "extant") copy?

This "bibliographic test" assesses the trustworthiness of any work of literature. It is based on the wise supposition that the more copies we can gather of a work—and the closer in time those copies are to the original—the greater our certainty that we possess the text as originally written.

To give us a basis for comparison, it is useful to consider how other ancient documents fare in this bibliographic test. Like the Bible, other works of ancient literature had to be copied over and over through the centuries to preserve them from loss through decay. Copies of classic works are often incomplete. They contain errors—slips of the pen, missing segments, misspelled words, and so on. These errors are often passed down through generations of copying. Having multiple copies available enables scholars to cross-check manuscripts and to determine the author's original words. The older the copies are the better, as older copies mean less time passed during which errors could be introduced and transmitted.

Surprisingly, few copies of most ancient writings still exist today. Modern editions of ancient books are often based on a mere handful of copies made centuries after the original composition. Virtually everything we know today about Julius Caesar's exploits in the Gallic Wars, for example, is derived from ten manuscript copies of *The Gallic Wars*, the earliest of which was produced about 1,000 years after the book was written. Our modern text of Livy's *History of Rome* relies on one partial manuscript and nineteen much later copies that are dated from 400 to 1,000 years after the original writing.[2]

Copies of other ancient works are similarly scarce. For example,

- Of fourteen books in the Histories of Tacitus (written about a.d. 100) only four and a half survive today. Of the sixteen books of his Annals, only ten survive in full. We derive the text for these two great historical works from only two manuscripts, one from the ninth century and one from the eleventh.

- The History of Thucydides (about 460–400 b.c.) comes to us from a few papyrus scraps from the early Christian era and eight manuscripts, the earliest from around a.d. 900.

• The comprehensive history of Rome by Velleius Paterculus survived to modern times in only one incomplete manuscript—and this lone manuscript was lost in the seventeenth century after being copied.

By comparison, the text of Homer's *Iliad* is much more reliable. It is supported by 643 manuscript copies in existence today, with a mere 400-year time gap between the date of composition and the earliest copies.

This information might tend to make non-scholars skeptical about the reliability of ancient literature. Yet as F. F. Bruce informs us, "No classical scholar would listen to an argument that the authenticity of Herodotus or Thucydides is in doubt because the earliest MSS [manuscripts] of their works which are of any use to us are over 1,300 years later than the originals."[3] Even working with scant evidence from these ancient documents, scholars are confident they can determine the authenticity and correct reading of the original document.

Scripture Stands Alone

If scholars judge the texts of these ancient works to be reliable with so little to work from, then we have enormous reason to trust that the Bible has been transmitted to us accurately. The textual evidence even for Homer's Iliad pales in comparison to the number of preserved copies of the New Testament text. Counting Greek copies alone, the New Testament is preserved in some 5,686 partial and complete manuscript portions that were copied by hand from the second through the fifteenth centuries.[4] And even more early texts of the New Testament are available to us today. Add to the nearly 5,700 Greek manuscripts more than 10,000 Latin Vulgate and at least 9,300 other early versions in additional languages, and we have close to 25,000 manuscript copies of portions of the New Testament in libraries and museums today. No other document of antiquity even begins to approach such numbers and thorough attestation.

Compared with nearly 5,700 Greek manuscripts of the New Testament, other ancient documents suffer a poverty of manuscripts, as the following chart demonstrates. [5]

Author/ Book	Date Written	Earliest Copies	Time Gap	No. of Copies
Homer, *Iliad*	800 B.C.	c. 400 b.c.	c. 400 yrs.	643
Herodotus, *History*	480–425 B.C.	C. A.D. 900	c. 1,350 yrs.	8
Thucydides, *History*	460–400 B.C.	C. A.D. 900	c. 1,300 yrs.	8
Plato	400 B.C.	C. A.D. 900	c.1,300 yrs.	7
Demosthenes	300 B.C.	C. A.D. 1100	c. 1,400 yrs.	200
Caesar, *Gallic Wars*	100–44 B.C.	C. A.D. 900	c. 1,000 yrs.	10
Livy, *History of Rome*	59 B.C.– A.D. 17	4th cent. (partial) mostly 10th cent.	c.400 yrs. c. 1,000 yrs.	1 partial 19 copies
Tacitus, *Annals*	A.D. 100	C. A.D. 1100	c. 1,000 yrs.	20
Pliny Secundus, *Natural History*	A.D. 61–113	C. A.D. 850	c. 750 yrs.	7
New Testament	A.D. 50–100	c. 114 (fragment) c. 200 (books) c. 250 (most of NT) c. 325 (complete NT)	+ 50 yrs. 100 yrs. 150 yrs. 225 yrs.	5366

British scholar and professor F. J. A. Hort rightly concludes that "in the variety and fullness of the evidence on which it rests the text of the New Testament stands absolutely and unapproachably alone among ancient prose writings."[6]

The importance of the sheer number of manuscript copies cannot be overstated. As with other documents of ancient literature, no original manuscripts of the Bible are known to exist. However, the abundance of manuscript copies makes it possible to reconstruct the original with virtually complete accuracy.[7] Bible scholars David S. Dockery, Kenneth A. Mathews, and

Robert B. Sloan have recently written, "For most of the biblical text a single reading has been transmitted. Elimination of scribal errors and intentional changes leaves only a small percentage of the text about which any questions occur."[8] They conclude, "Although there are certainly differences in many of the New Testament manuscripts, not one fundamental doctrine of the Christian faith rests on a disputed reading."[9]

Closing the Gap

The New Testament not only rises above other ancient literature in the quantity of surviving manuscripts; it also surpasses all others in the second test of any ancient work—the gap of time measured between the writing of a text and the earliest known manuscripts. The earliest portion of the New Testament is not a millennium or more away from the hand of its author; a fragment of John's gospel currently housed in the John Rylands Library of Manchester, England, has been determined to be within fifty years of the date when the apostle John penned the original.

In fact, the gap between the autograph (the original manuscript) and the oldest extant manuscript is far less for the New Testament than for any other known work in Greek literature. Sir Frederic G. Kenyon, director and principal librarian of the British Museum and second to none in authority for evaluating manuscripts, summarizes how the textual basis of the New Testament contrasts with that of other classical documents:

> In no other case is the interval of time between the composition of the book and the date of the earliest extant manuscripts so short as in that of the New Testament. The books of the New Testament were written in the latter part of the first century; the earliest extant manuscripts (trifling scraps excepted) are of the fourth century—say from 250 to 300 years later. This may sound a considerable interval, but it is nothing to that which parts most of the great classical

authors from their earliest manuscripts. We believe that we have in all essentials an accurate text of the seven extant plays of Sophocles; yet the earliest substantial manuscript upon which it is based was written more than 1400 years after the poet's death.[10]

Kenyon continues in *The Bible and Archaeology*: "The interval then between the dates of original composition and the earliest extant evidence becomes so small as to be in fact negligible, and the last foundation for any doubt that the Scriptures have come down to us substantially as they were written has now been removed. Both the authenticity and the general integrity of the books of the New Testament may be regarded as finally established."[11]

This fact is detailed in the following chart:

Textual Reliability Standards Applied to the Bible					
Author	**Book**	**Date Written**	**Earliest Copies**	**Time Gap**	**No. of Copies**
John	New Testament	A.D. 50–100	C. A.D. 130	+ 50 yrs.	Fragments
The rest of the New Testament authors			C. A.D. 200 (Books)	100 yrs.	
			C. A.D. 250 (Most of N.T.)	150 yrs.	
			C. A.D. 325 (Complete N.T.)	225 yrs.	+5,600 Greek Mss.
			C. A.D. 366–384 (Latin Vulgate Trans.)	284 yrs.	
			C. A.D. 400–500 (Other Trans.)	400 yrs.	+19,000 Trans. Mss.
			TOTALS	**50–400 yrs.**	**+24,900 Mss.**

No wonder speaker and Christian apologist Ravi Zacharias concludes, "In real terms, the New Testament is easily the best attested ancient writing in terms of the sheer number of documents, the time span between the events and the document, and the variety of documents available to sustain or contradict it. There is nothing in ancient manuscript evidence to match such textual availability and integrity."[12]

The Reliability of the Old Testament

The internal evidence for the reliability of the New Testament is convincing and compelling, but what about the Old Testament? The Old Testament text is vitally related to the New Testament. Its reliability supports the Christian faith, not only in establishing the dates when supernatural predictions were made of the Messiah but also in supporting the historicity of the Old Testament that Jesus and New Testament writers affirmed.[13]

How can we know that the original words of the Old Testament survived intact through centuries even further removed from us than the New Testament? While the New Testament is renowned for the sheer number and age of manuscripts that survived to modern times, the Old Testament's reliability is underscored by our knowledge of the meticulous methods of the scribes who copied the manuscripts from generation to generation and whose work we can check for accuracy against manuscripts that lay undisturbed for almost two millennia.

God commanded and instilled in the Jewish people a great reverence for his Word. From their very first days as a nation, God told them, "Listen closely, Israel, to everything I say . . . Commit yourselves wholeheartedly to these commands I am giving you today. Repeat them again and again to your children. Talk about them when you are at home and when you are away on a journey, when you are lying down and when you are getting up again. Tie them to your hands as a reminder, and wear them on your forehead. Write them on the doorposts of your house and on your gates" (Deuteronomy 6:3, 6–9, NLT).

That attitude toward the commands of God became such a part of the Jewish identity that a class of Jewish scholars called the

Sopherim, from a Hebrew word meaning "scribes," arose between the fifth and third centuries b.c. The Sopherim became custodians of the Hebrew Scriptures and dedicated themselves to preserving the ancient manuscripts and producing new copies when necessary.

The Sopherim were superceded by the Talmudic scribes, who guarded, interpreted, and commented on the sacred texts from a.d. 100–500. In turn, the Talmudic scribes were followed by the better-known Masoretic scribes (a.d. 500–900).

The zeal of the Masoretes (from *masora*, "tradition") surpassed that of even their most dedicated predecessors. They established detailed and stringent disciplines for copying a manuscript. With their headquarters in Tiberias, the text that the Masoretes preserved is called the "Masoretic" Text. The Masoretes' rules were so rigorous that when a new copy was complete they would give the reproduction equal authority to that of its parent because they were thoroughly convinced that they had an exact duplicate. The Masoretic Text is the standard Hebrew text for the Old Testament today.

God's Meticulous Scribes

The Masoretes had such a painstaking reverence for the Hebrew Scriptures that they formulated a stringent set of rules to preserve the holiness of their approach to their work and ensure the accuracy of it. A scribe began his day of transcribing by ceremonially washing his entire body. He then dressed himself in full Jewish attire before sitting at his desk to write. When he wrote the Hebrew name of God, he could not begin with a quill newly dipped in ink for fear it would smear the page. Once he began writing the name of God, he could not stop or allow himself to be distracted. Even if a king entered the room, the scribe was obligated to continue without interruption until he finished penning the holy name of the one true God.

The Masoretic guidelines for copying manuscripts also required the following:

- The scroll must be written on the skin of a clean animal.

- Each skin must contain a specified number of columns, equal throughout the entire book.

- The length of each column must extend no less than forty-eight lines or more than sixty lines.

- The column breadth must consist of exactly thirty letters.

- The space of a thread must appear between every consonant.

- The breadth of nine consonants had to be inserted between each section.

- A space of three lines had to appear between each book.

- The fifth book of Moses (Deuteronomy) had to conclude exactly with a full line.

- Nothing—not even the shortest word—could be copied from memory; it had to be copied letter by letter.

- The scribe must count the number of times each letter of the alphabet occurred in each book and compare it to the original.

- If a manuscript was found to contain even one mistake, it was discarded.[14]

Not only were the Masoretes reverent and well-disciplined, but they devised a complicated system of safeguards against scribal slips. They counted, for example, the number of times each letter of the alphabet occurs in each book; they pointed out the middle letter of the Pentateuch and the middle letter of the whole Hebrew Bible and made even more detailed calculations than these. "Everything countable seems to be counted," says Wheeler Robinson, and they made up mnemonics by which the various totals might be readily remembered.[15]

The scribes could tell if one consonant was left out of, say, the entire book of Isaiah or the entire Hebrew Bible. Because of these many and meticulous safeguards, they knew when they finished that they had an exact copy. Sir Frederic Kenyon says,

Besides recording varieties of reading, tradition, or conjecture, the Masoretes undertook a number of calculations which do not enter into the ordinary sphere of textual criticism. They numbered the verses, words, and letters of every book. They calculated the middle word and the middle letter of each. They enumerated verses which contained all the letters of the alphabet, or a certain number of them. These trivialities, as we may rightly consider them, had yet the effect of securing minute attention to the precise transmission of the text; and they are but an excessive manifestation of a respect for the sacred Scriptures which in itself deserves nothing but praise. The Masoretes were indeed anxious that not one jot nor tittle, not one smallest letter nor one tiny part of a letter of the Law should pass away or be lost.[16]

The Dead Sea Scrolls: A Priceless Double Check

While the great skill and care of the Masorite scribes is nothing short of awe-inspiring, we had no way of knowing until recently just how totally their dedication translated into accuracy. Confirmation came with a discovery off the shores of Israel's Dead Sea.

In the spring of 1947, a Bedouin shepherd boy named Muhammad was searching for a lost goat. As Ralph Earle summarizes the story, "He tossed a stone into a hole in a cliff on the west side of the Dead Sea, about eight miles south of Jericho. To his surprise he heard the sound of shattering pottery. Investigating, he discovered an amazing sight. On the floor of the cave were several large jars containing leather scrolls, wrapped in linen cloth."[17] The jars were carefully sealed, and the scrolls evidently placed there in a.d. 68 had been preserved in excellent condition for nearly 1,900 years.

The Dead Sea Scrolls comprise some forty thousand written fragments. From these fragments more than five hundred books have been reconstructed. Many extrabiblical books and fragments were discovered that shed light on the second century b.c. to the first century a.d. religious community of Qumran on the shores of the Dead Sea. But the most important documents in the Dead Sea Scrolls are copies of the Old Testament text dating from more than a century before the birth of Christ. Before 1947, the oldest complete Hebrew manuscript dated to a.d. 900. But with the discovery of 223 manuscripts in these caves, we now have Old Testament manuscripts that have been dated by paleographers at as early as 125 b.c.—more than a thousand years older than any manuscript previously possessed.

Before the discovery of the Dead Sea Scrolls, scholars could not with certainty answer the big question: "Because the Old Testament text has been copied over so many times, can we trust it?" The Dead Sea Scrolls provided an emphatic answer. They gave scholars a way to double-check the accuracy of later Old Testament copies. And the double check confirmed that a thousand years of copying the Scriptures had produced only insignificant variations, none of which affected the meaning of the text. The Hebrew Bible found in the Dead Sea Scrolls proved to be identical, word for word, in more than ninety-five percent of the text. (The variation of five percent consisted mainly of spelling variations.)[18]

The discovery of the Dead Sea Scrolls demonstrates the meticulous accuracy of the copyists of the Scripture over a thousand-year period, from the copying of the Isaiah scroll (125 b.c.) to the Masoretic Text of Isaiah (a.d. 916).

In conclusion, we can see that the Masorite scribes and their predecessors gave the most diligent attention to accurate preservation of the Hebrew Scriptures that has ever been devoted to any work of ancient literature, secular or religious, in the history of human civilization. Because of their faithfulness, we have today a form of the Hebrew Bible which in all essentials duplicates the text which was considered authoritative in the days of Christ and the apostles and even a century earlier. As W. F. Albright has said, "We may rest assured that the consonantal text of the Hebrew Bible, though not infallible, has been preserved with an accuracy perhaps unparalleled in any other Near Eastern literature."[19]

Conclusion

Edward Glenny, Professor of Biblical Studies at Northwestern College, raises an important point for those of us concerned about the reliability of the text of the Bible: "No one questions the authenticity of the historical books of antiquity because we do not possess the original copies," and yet, he adds, "We have far fewer manuscripts of these works than we possess of the NT."[20]

The difference between the Bible and other ancient works in the quantity and quality of texts is so great that John Warwick Montgomery says that "to be skeptical of the resultant text of the New Testament books is to allow all of classical antiquity to slip into obscurity, for no documents of the ancient period are as well attested bibliographically as the New Testament."[21]

The thousands of Hebrew manuscripts, with their confirmation by the Septuagint and the Samaritan Pentateuch, and the numerous other cross-checks from outside and inside the text provide overwhelming support for the reliability of the Old Testament text. Therefore, it is appropriate to conclude with Kenyon's statement, "The Christian can take the whole Bible in his hand and say without fear or hesitation that he holds in it the true word of God, handed down without essential loss from generation to generation throughout the centuries."[22]

From the moment the authors of Scripture lifted pen from paper, skeptics have tried to refute the Bible, unbelievers have tried to stamp it out, and despots have tried to burn it. However, Scripture has not only prevailed but also proliferated. Voltaire, the noted eighteenth-century French skeptic, predicted that within a hundred years of his time Christianity would be but a footnote in history. Ironically, in 1828, fifty years after Voltaire's death, the Geneva Bible Society moved into his house and used his printing press to produce thousands of Bibles to distribute worldwide. Voltaire unknowingly bowed to the words of Isaiah the prophet, who said, "People are like the grass that dies away . . . but the word of our God stands forever."[21]

CHAPTER 4

The Bible Is Reliable: External Evidence

In the last two chapters, we examined samplings of the evidence showing that the Bible is amazingly accurate both in its original recording and in its transmission to us over the centuries. Yet we have even more evidence for the Bible's reliability. We have data from outside Scripture confirming the truth of what is written in Scripture. In addition to examining a document's internal and bibliographic reliability, this external reinforcement is the third test for accuracy that scholars apply to historical documents. This test determines whether other historical material confirms or conflicts with the internal testimony of the document itself. In other words, can writings be found apart from the literature under analysis that substantiate its accuracy, reliability, and authenticity?

External sources reinforce the Bible at least as strongly as they reinforce other works of ancient literature. We have persuasive external evidence of the Bible's reliability from three outside sources—the writings of early Christians, the works of non-Christian writers from the first few centuries a.d., and the testimony of archaeology to the authenticity of both the Old and New Testaments. Mountains of such evidence exist, and I can give you only a sampling here. For a more complete and thorough examination of these evidences, I refer you to my book, *The New Evidence that Demands a Verdict*, from which most of the material in this chapter is condensed.

Evidence from the Writings of Early Christians

Since the time of its first composition, the Bible has been by far the most widely referenced and quoted book in all of history. Leaders, writers, and theologians in the early church often quoted extensive passages from the gospels and epistles of the New Testament. While some of these quotations were not word-for-word, they nonetheless serve an indispensable role as external evidence to the content of Scripture.[1] As theologian and educator Norman Geisler explains,

> The writings of the most authoritative writers of the early church—the leaders scholars refer to collectively as the Apostolic Fathers—give overwhelming support to the existence of the twenty-seven authoritative books of the New Testament. Some Apostolic Fathers produced extensive, highly accurate quotes from the text of the New Testament . . . Early Christian writers provide quotations so numerous and widespread that if no manuscripts of the New Testament existed today, 'the New Testament could be reproduced from the writings of the early Fathers alone.'[2]

Geisler and theologian/professor William Nix tell us that "there were some 32,000 citations of the New Testament prior to the time of the Council of Nicea (a.d. 325). These 32,000 quotations are by no means exhaustive, and they do not even include the fourth-century writers. Just adding the number of references used by one other writer, Eusebius, who flourished prior to and contemporary with the Council at Nicea, brings the total number of citations of the New Testament to over 36,000."[3] Geisler's chart below provides a graphic summary of these quotes:[4]

Early Citations of the New Testament						
Writer	Gospels	Acts	Pauline Epistles	General Epistles	Revelation	Totals
Justin Martyr	268	10	43	6	3	330
						(266 allusions)
Irenaeus	1,038	194	499	23	65	1,819
Clement Alex.	1,107	44	1,127	207	11	2,406
Origen	9,231	349	7,778	399	165	17,992
Tertullian	3,822	502	2,609	120	205	7,258
Hippolytus	734	42	387	27	188	1,378
Eusebius	3,258	211	1,592	88	27	5,176
Grand Totals	19,368	1,352	14,035	870	664	36,289

These were not the only writers who quoted the New Testament extensively. Many other voices in the early church bore witness to the New Testament manuscripts. Among them:

- **Clement of Rome** (a.d. 95) quotes from Matthew, Mark, Luke, Acts, 1 Corinthians, 1 Peter, Hebrews, and Titus.

- **Ignatius** (a.d. 70–110), Bishop of Antioch, knew the apostles firsthand. His seven letters contain quotations from thirteen New Testament books, including Matthew, John, Acts, Romans, Galatians, James, and 1 Peter.

- **Clement of Alexandria** (a.d. 150–212). His 2,400 quotes derive from all but three books of the New Testament.

- **Cyprian** (died a.d. 258), bishop of Carthage, uses approximately 740 Old Testament citations and 1,030 from the New Testament.

Besides providing us with a testimony to the text of the New Testament, early Christian writers give us tantalizing glimpses of the remarkable care taken in the writing of the biblical accounts of Christ.

- **Eusebius** records comments that ultimately can be traced back to "the Elder" (the apostle John) via the writings of Papias, bishop of Heirapolis (a.d. 130). Papias reports John's words that Mark, though not a follower of Christ, "wrote down accurately all that he (Peter) mentioned, whether sayings or doings of Christ." And "Mark made no mistake writing down in this way some things as he (Peter) mentioned them; for he paid attention to this one thing, not to omit anything that he had heard, not to include any false statement among them."[5]

- **Irenaeus,** Bishop of Lyons, had been a Christian for eighty-six years when he was martyred in a.d. 156. As a disciple of John the Apostle he was in an excellent position to verify the accounts of Jesus. He writes,

  Matthew published his gospel among the Hebrews (i.e., Jews) in their own tongue, when Peter and Paul were preaching the gospel in Rome and founding the church there. After their departure (i.e., their death, which strong tradition places at the time of the Neronian persecution in 64), Mark, the disciple and interpreter of Peter, himself handed down to us in writing the substance of Peter's preaching. Luke, the follower of Paul, set down in a book the gospel preached by his teacher. Then John, the disciple of the Lord, who also leaned on His breast (this is a reference to John 13:25 and 21:20), himself produced his gospel, while he was living at Ephesus in Asia.[6]

These early quotations give evidence not only of the existence of the original New Testament documents, but their consistency reinforces evidence of their content.

Evidence from Early Non-Christian Writers

The evidence supporting the New Testament from early Christian writers is excellent, but it is not all we have. In addition, many non-Christians from early centuries confirmed the people, places, and events of the New Testament in their own writings. Surveying the works of these other ancient writers yields abundant external confirmation that the world at large was well aware of the events of the New Testament and the claims laid out in Scripture. Consider these notable examples:

• **Tacitus,** a first-century Roman, is considered one of the most accurate historians of the ancient world. Here is his account of the great fire of Rome, for which some blamed the emperor Nero:

Consequently, to get rid of the report, Nero fastened the guilt and inflicted the most exquisite tortures on a class hated for their abominations, called Christians by the populace. Christus, from whom the name had its origin, suffered the extreme penalty during the reign of Tiberius at the hands of one of our procurators, Pontius Pilatus, and a most mischievous superstition, thus checked for the moment, again broke out not only in Judea, the first source of the evil, but even in Rome, where all things hideous and shameful from every part of the world find their center and become popular.[7]

The "mischievous superstition" to which Tacitus refers is most likely the resurrection of Jesus. The same is true for one of the references made by Suetonius below.

- **Suetonius** was chief secretary to Emperor Hadrian, who reigned in Rome from a.d. 117–138. He confirms the report in Acts 18:2 that Claudius commanded all Jews to leave Rome in a.d. 49.[8] Speaking of the aftermath of the great fire at Rome, Suetonius reports, "Punishment was inflicted on the Christians, a body of people addicted to a novel and mischievous superstition."[9]

- **Josephus** (c. a.d. 37–c. a.d. 100) was a Pharisee of the priestly line and a Jewish historian. His writings contain many statements that verify the historical nature of both the Old and New Testaments. Josephus refers to Jesus as the brother of James who was martyred. He writes that the high priest, Ananias, "assembled the Sanhedrin of the judges, and brought before them the brother of Jesus, who was called Christ, whose name was James, and some others, and when he had formed an accusation against them as breakers of the law, he delivered them to be stoned."[10] This passage, written in a.d. 93, confirms in the first century the New Testament reports that Jesus was a real person, that he was identified by others as the Christ, and that he had a brother named James who died a martyr's death at the hands of the high priest and his Sanhedrin.

- **Thallus** wrote around a.d. 52. In about a.d. 221, Julius Africanus quotes Thallus in a discussion about the darkness that followed the crucifixion of Christ: "On the whole world there pressed a most fearful darkness, and the rocks were rent by an earthquake, and many places in Judea and other districts were thrown down."[11]

- Pliny the Younger was a Roman author and administrator with access to official information not available to the public. In a letter to the Emperor Trajan in about a.d. 112, Pliny describes the early Christian worship practices:

> They were in the habit of meeting on a certain fixed day before it was light, when they sang in alternate verses a hymn to Christ, as to a god, and bound themselves by a solemn oath, not to do any wicked deeds, but never to commit any fraud, theft or adultery, never to falsify their word, nor deny a trust when they should be called upon to deliver it up; after which it was their custom to separate, and then reassemble to partake of food—but food of an ordinary and innocent kind.[12]

This reference provides solid evidence that Jesus Christ was worshiped as God from an early date by Christians who continued to follow the practice of breaking bread together, as reported in Acts 2:42 and in verse forty-six.

- **Emperor Trajan,** in a reply to Pliny's letter, gave the following guidelines for punishing Christians: "No search should be made for these people; when they are denounced and found guilty they must be punished, with the restriction, however, that when the party denies himself to be a Christian, and shall give proof that he is not (that is, by adoring our gods) he shall be pardoned on the ground of repentance even though he may have formerly incurred suspicion."[13]

- **Lucian of Samosata** was a second-century Greek writer whose works contain sarcastic critiques of Christianity. Lucian wrote,

> The Christians, you know, worship a man to this day—
> the distinguished personage who introduced their novel

rites, and was crucified on that account . . . You see, these misguided creatures start with the general conviction that they are immortal for all time, which explains the contempt of death and voluntary self-devotion which are so common among them; and then it was impressed on them by their original lawgiver that they are all brothers, from the moment that they are converted, and deny the gods of Greece, and worship the crucified sage, and live after his laws. All this they take quite on faith, with the result that they despise all worldly goods alike, regarding them merely as common property.[14]

Gary Habermas, a leading researcher and writer on the historical events surrounding Jesus, lists several verified facts that can be ascertained from this text: "Jesus was worshiped by Christians . . . Jesus introduced new teachings in Palestine . . . He was crucified because of these teachings . . . such as all believers are brothers, from the moment that conversion takes place, and after the false gods are denied . . . [Also] these teachings included worshiping Jesus and living according to his laws."[15] Habermas adds, "Concerning Christians, we are told that they are followers of Jesus who believe themselves to be immortal . . . [They] accepted Jesus' teachings by faith and practiced their faith by their disregard for material possessions."[16]

Summing Up These Contributions

What is the value of these non-Christian references to Jesus? Geisler summarizes,

"The primary sources for the life of Christ are the four Gospels. However there are considerable reports from non-Christian sources that supplement and confirm the Gospel accounts. These come largely from Greek, Roman, Jewish, and Samaritan sources of the first century. In brief they inform us that:

1. Jesus was from Nazareth.

2. He lived a wise and virtuous life.

3. He was crucified in Palestine under Pontius Pilate during the reign of Tiberius Caesar at Passover time, being considered the Jewish King.

4. He was believed by his disciples to have been raised from the dead three days later.

5. His enemies acknowledged that he performed unusual feats they called 'sorcery.'

6. His small band of disciples multiplied rapidly, spreading even as far as Rome.

7. His disciples denied polytheism, lived moral lives, and worshiped Christ as Divine.

This picture confirms the view of Christ presented in the New Testament Gospels."[17]

These and other outside sources give more substantiation for the accuracy of the biblical record than for any other book in history. Dr. Habermas adds a point that many overlook: "We should realize that it is quite extraordinary that we could provide a broad outline of most of the major facts of Jesus' life from 'secular' history alone. Such is surely significant."[18]

Evidence from Archaeology

Quotes and references from ancient literature are not the only external evidences that support the Bible's reliability. Over and over again, especially in the last half-century, archaeological discoveries have strongly affirmed the biblical record. In the nineteenth and early twentieth centuries, the silence of the archaeological record was used as evidence against the Bible, but since then numerous finds have confirmed the historical accuracy and careful precision of both Old and New Testament writers. As a result, scholars are increasingly realizing that the historical parts of the Bible must be regarded as reliable accounts of factual information. W. F. Albright, archaeologist and Professor of Semitic Languages at Johns Hopkins University, says: "The excessive skepticism shown toward the Bible by important historical schools of the eighteenth and nineteenth centuries, certain phases of which still appear periodically, has been progressively discredited. Discovery after discovery has established the accuracy of innumerable details, and has brought increased recognition to the value of the Bible as a source of history." [19]

Here is a single example: Until 1961 no archaeological evidence had been discovered to support the existence of Pontius Pilate. That year two Italian archaeologists uncovered a Latin inscription referring to the Roman governor.

Scholars from many disciplines have recognized that archaeology has never shown Scripture to be false. As reformed Jewish scholar Nelson Glueck observed, "It may be stated categorically that no archaeological discovery has ever controverted a biblical reference."[20]

It would take many volumes to contain all the finds that have undergirded the historical reliability of the Bible. In the next two sections of this chapter, I will give just a few samplings from the discoveries of eminent archaeologists and their opinions regarding the implications of those finds for both the New and Old Testaments.

Archaeology and the New Testament

Archaeology underscored the reliability of the New Testament in a most spectacular way when it confirmed the absolute accuracy of Luke's accounts in his gospel and the book of Acts. At one time critics concluded that in Luke's detailed report of the birth of Jesus (Luke 2:1–3), his facts were badly garbled: that there was no census; that Quirinius was not governor of Syria at that time; and that citizens were not required to return to their ancestral homes to be counted.[21]

But subsequent archaeological discoveries confirmed Luke's history. First, they showed that the Romans did have a regular enrollment of taxpayers and conducted censuses every fourteen years. This procedure was indeed begun under Augustus, and the first took place in either 23–22 b.c. or in 9–8 b.c. The latter would be the one to which Luke refers. Second, an inscription found in Antioch confirmed that Quirinius was governor of Syria around 7 b.c.[22] Third, a papyrus found in Egypt gives directions for the conduct of a Roman census. It reads, "Because of the approaching census it is necessary that all those residing for any cause away from their homes should at once prepare to return to their own governments in order that they may complete the family registration of the enrollment and that the tilled lands may retain those belonging to them."[23]

Research has also laid to rest all doubts about Luke's accuracy in geography, language, and culture. Archaeologists once believed he was dead wrong in placing the cities of Lystra and Derbe in Lycaonia, and Iconium outside it (Acts 14:6, 19). Since the writings of the Roman Cicero indicated that Iconium was in Lycaonia, Archaeologists concluded that the book of Acts was unreliable. However, in 1910, British archaeologist Sir William Ramsay found a monument showing that Iconium was a Phrygian city, a discovery later confirmed by other finds.[24] Many additional archaeological discoveries have identified most of the ancient cities mentioned in the book of Acts. As a result, the journeys of Paul can now be accurately traced.[25] Geisler tells us that Luke names thirty-two countries, fifty-four cities, and nine islands without error.[26]

Linguists doubted Luke's usage of certain words. A classic case is his denoting the civil authorities of Thessalonica as *politarchs* (Acts 17:6). Since *politarch* isn't found in classical literature, Luke was again assumed to be wrong. However, some nineteen inscriptions containing the title have since been found.[27]

Historians questioned Luke's account of the riot of Ephesus where he described the event as a civic assembly (Ecclesia) that took place in an amphitheater (Acts 19:23–29). But Luke was proved right again when an inscription was found telling of silver statues of Artemis to be placed in the "theater during a full session of the *Ecclesia*." The theater, when excavated, proved to have room for twenty-five thousand people.

Luke also relates that a riot broke out in Jerusalem because Paul took a Gentile into the temple (Acts 21:28). Inscriptions have been found in both Greek and Latin reading, "No foreigner may enter within the barrier which surrounds the temple and enclosure. Anyone who is caught doing so will be personally responsible for his ensuing death." Luke is vindicated again.[28]

Colin Hemer, a noted Roman historian, has catalogued numerous archaeological and historical confirmations of Luke's accuracy in his book *The Book of Acts in the Setting of Hellenistic History*. Following is a summary of just five points of his voluminous, detailed report. He shows that the book of Acts is confirmed by the following:

1. Specialized details, which would not have been widely known except to a contemporary researcher such as Luke who traveled widely. These details include exact titles of officials, identification of army units, and information about major routes.

2. Details archaeologists know to be accurate but can't verify as to the precise time period. Some of these are unlikely to have been known except to a writer who had visited the districts.

3. Correlation of dates of known kings and governors with the chronology of the narrative.

4. "Undesigned coincidents" between Acts and the Pauline Epistles.

5. Cultural or idiomatic items now known to be peculiar to the first-century atmosphere.[29]

Luke's reliability as a historian is unquestionable. Roman historian A. N. Sherwin-White writes, "For Acts the confirmation of historicity is overwhelming . . . Any attempt to reject its basic historicity must now appear absurd. Roman historians have long taken it for granted."[30] E. M. Blaiklock, professor of classics at Auckland University, concludes that "Luke is a consummate historian, to be ranked in his own right with the great writers of the Greeks."[31]

Archaeology and the Old Testament

Archaeology provides invaluable support of the reliability of the Old Testament as well as the New. Discoveries enhance our knowledge of its economic, cultural, social, and political background and confirm the existence of people once thought by critics to be mere legend. Until recently, says Albright, whose reputation places him among the greatest of archaeologists, biblical critics regarded the Old Testament accounts of the patriarchs as the products of Israelite scribes or campfire storytellers. Historians had discounted almost every person and event of Genesis.[32] However, Albright tells us that "Archaeological discoveries since 1925 have changed all this. Aside from a few diehards among older scholars, there is scarcely a single biblical historian who has not been impressed by the rapid accumulation of data supporting the substantial historicity of patriarchal tradition."[33]

Consider the following selected examples of how archaeological discoveries have substantiated key narratives in the Old Testament:

Sodom and Gomorrah

The destruction of Sodom and Gomorrah was regarded as religious legend until evidence revealed that all five of the cities mentioned as allies of Sodom in Genesis fourteen were in fact centers of commerce in the area and were geographically situated as the Scriptures describe. The biblical description of their destruction appears to be just as accurate. Evidence in the area points to ancient earthquake activity disrupting the layers of the earth and hurling them high into the air. In addition the evidence indicates that the present layers of sedimentary rock have been molded together by intense heat, pointing to a great conflagration that took place possibly when an oil basin beneath the Dead Sea ignited and erupted. Bitumen is plentiful on the site, and an accurate description of the event would be that brimstone (bituminous pitch) was hurled down on those cities.[34]

Jericho

During the excavations of Jericho (1930–1936) British archaeologist John Garstang found something so startling that he and two other members of the team prepared and signed a statement describing it. Garstang says, "there remains no doubt: the walls fell outwards so completely that the attackers would be able to clamber up and over their ruins into the city." Why is this so unusual? Because the walls of besieged cities don't fall outwards; they fall inwards, forced by the attackers. Garstang's find confirms what we read in Joshua 6:20 (NLT): "Suddenly, the walls of Jericho collapsed, and the Israelites charged straight into the city from every side and captured it."[35]

David

Critics once thought David to be a legendary king mentioned nowhere else but in the Bible. But a 1994 discovery—an inscription from the ninth-century b.c.e. refers to both the House of David and to the King of Israel.[36]

Belshazzar

Daniel's mention of the last Babylonian king, Belshazzar (Daniel 5), was once thought to be a mistake, since a tablet named Nabonidus, not Belshazzar, as the last king of Babylon. However, later discoveries confirmed that Belshazzar, the son of Nabonidus, ruled as coregent with his father.

As these samplings of evidence show, in every period of Bible history, the findings of archaeology attest that the Scriptures speak the truth.

Conclusion

All external evidence—the writings of early Christians, the writings of early non-Christians, and the findings of archaeology—give resounding evidence that the entire Bible, both Old and New Testaments, are utterly reliable historically. In fact, these few samplings I have selected for this chapter from the mountains of available evidence show us that the Bible is the most thoroughly documented and reinforced set of writings in all antiquity. This proven trustworthiness on testable historical information gives us strong reason to believe the Bible is just as trustworthy in its doctrines, its accounts of the activity of God, and its claims about the deity, life, death, and resurrection of Jesus. Clearly the Bible as a whole is altogether reliable, and we can trust it as an introduction to our relational God. We can trust its promises of protection and provision for those who seek a relationship with him.

Notes

CHAPTER *1*

1. Josephson Institute of Ethics, "The Ethics of American Youth," *2002ReportCard* http://www.josephsoninstitute.org.
2. George Barna, *Think Like Jesus* (Grand Rapids: Baker Books, 2003), 26.
3. C.S. Lewis, *George MacDonald Anthology* (London: Geoffrey Bles, 1946), 25.

CHAPTER *2*

1. James Weldon Johnson, *God's Trombones* (New York: Penguin Books, 1927), 17.

CHAPTER *3*

1. Andy Harrington, "Who Stole My Rule Book?" *Youthworker Journal*, CCM Communications, November/December 2002.

CHAPTER *8*

1. Bob Hostetler and Josh McDowell, *The New Tolerance* (Wheaton, Illinois: Tyndale House, 1998), 94.

CHAPTER *9*

1. C.S. Lewis, *The Weight of Glory and Other Addresses* (New York: Macmillan Publishing Co., Inc., 1949), 18–19.
2. Charles Caldwell Ryrie, ed., *Ryrie Study Bible* (Chicago: Moody Press, 1976), 25.

CHAPTER *10*

1. C.S. Lewis, *The Four Loves* (New York: Harcourt, Brace & World, 1960).
2. M. J. Rutter, "Developmental catch-up, and deficit, following adoption after severe global early privation," *Child Psychiatry* 39 (1998): 465–76.
3. Kevin Leman, *Becoming the Parent God Wants You to Be* (Colorado Springs: NavPress Publishing Group, 1998), 86.
4. Kathleen Fury, "Sex and the American Teenager," *Ladies Home Journal*, March 1986.
5. Quoted from Josh McDowell, *The Disconnected Generation* (Nashville: Word Publishing, 2000), 99.
6. Armand Nicholi Jr., "Changes in the American Family," *White House Paper*, October 25, 1984, 7–8.

CHAPTER 13

1. The Newsletter of the American Academy of Matrimonial Lawyers, summer 1997.
2. Tim Rotheisler, *Alberta Report*, August 4, 1997.
3. John Donne, *Meditation XVII*.
4. Rafe VanHoy, *"What's Forever For"* (New York: Tree Publishing Co., 1978).

CHAPTER 14

1. Barna Research Group, "Third Millennium Teens" (Ventura, CA: The Barna Research Group, Ltd., 1999), 44.
2. Ibid., 43.

CHAPTER 15

1. 1994 Josh McDowell Church Youth Study analysis, cited in McDowell and Hostetler, *Right from Wrong*, (Nashville: W Publishing Group, 1994), 255–256.
2. Ibid. 255–256.

Bonus Resource

CHAPTER 1

1. See Josh McDowell, *More Than a Carpenter* (Wheaton, IL: Tyndale House, 1977), and McDowell, *The New Evidence That Demands a Verdict* (Nashville: Thomas Nelson Publishers, 1999).

CHAPTER 2

1. *The Random House College Dictionary* (New York: Random House, 1980), 1412.
2. John Warwick Montgomery, *Essays in Evidential Apologetics* (Nashville: Thomas Nelson, 1978), 29.
3. Robert M. Horn, *The Book That Speaks for Itself* (Downers Grove: InterVarsity Press, 1970), 86–87.
4. Gleason L. Archer, Jr., *Encyclopedia of Bible Difficulties* (Grand Rapids: Zondervan, 1982), 12.
5. Norman L. Geisler and Thomas A. Howe, *When Critics Ask* (Wheaton: Victor Books, 1992), 15–26.
6. Rose Arce and Shannon Troetel, reporters, "Top New York Times Editors Quit," CNN.com, March 1, 2004.
7. F. F. Bruce, *The New Testament Documents: Are They Reliable?* (Downers Grove: InterVarsity, 1964), 44–46.

8. Ibid., 33,44–46.

9. Ibid., 33,44–46.

10. W. F. Albright, *Recent Discoveries in Bible Lands* (New York: Funk and Wagnalls, 1955), 136.

11. William F. Albright, "Toward a More Conservative View," interview in *Christianity Today*, vol. VII, January 18, 1963: 8.

12. W. F. Albright, *From the Stone Age to Christianity* (Baltimore: Johns Hopkins Press, 1940), 23.

13. John Warwick Montgomery, *History and Christianity* (Downers Grove: InterVarsity, 1964), 34–35.

14. John A. T. Robinson, *Redating the New Testamant* (Philadelphia: Westminster, 1976).

CHAPTER 3

1. Bible figures from United Bible Society, *2005 Scripture Distribution Report*, http:// www.biblesociety.org/index2.htm.

2. F. F. Bruce, *The New Testament Documents: Are They Reliable?* (Downers Grove: InterVarsity, 1964), 16.

3. Ibid., 16-17.

4. Norman L. Geisler, *A General Introduction to the Bible* (Chicago: Moody Press, 1968), 385.

5. Ibid., 408.

6. F. J. A. Hort, and Brooke Foss Westcott, *The New Testament in the Original Greek*, vol. 1 (New York: Macmillan, 1881), 561.

7. Geisler, *A General Introduction to the Bible*, 386.

8. David S. Dockery, Kenneth A. Mathews, Robert B. Sloan, *Foundations for Biblical Interpretation* (Nashville: Broadman & Holman, 1994), 176.

9. Ibid., 182.

10. Frederic G. Kenyon, *Handbook to the Textual Criticism of the New Testament* (London: Macmillan, 1901), 4.

11. Frederic G. Kenyon, *The Bible and Archaeology* (New York: Harper and Row, 1940), 288.

12. Ravi Zacharias, *Can Man Live Without God?* (Nashville: W Publishing, 1994), 162.

13. Norman L. Geisler, *Baker Encyclopedia of Christian Apologetics* (Grand Rapids: Baker, 1998), 552–553.

14. Norman L. Geisler and William E. Nix, *A General Introduction to the Bible* (Chicago: Moody Press, 1968), 241.

15. F. F. Bruce, *The Books and the Parchments: How We Got Our English Bible* (Old Tappan: Fleming H. Revell, 1984), 117.

16. Frederic G. Kenyon, *Our Bible and the Ancient Manuscripts* (London: Eyre and Spottiswoode, 1939), 38.

17. Ralph Earle, *How We Got Our Bible* (Grand Rapids: Baker Book House, 1971), 48-49.

18. Gleason L. Archer Jr., *A Survey of Old Testament Introduction* (Chicago: Moody Press, 1964, 1974), 25.

19. W.F. Albright, quoted in Gleason L. Archer Jr., *A Survey of Old Testament Introduction* (Chicago: Moody Press, 1964), 65.

20. W. Edward Glenny, "The Preservation of Scripture" in *The Bible Version Debate* (Minneapolis: Central Baptist Theological Seminary, 1997), 96.

21. John Warwick Montgomery, *History and Christianity* (Downers Grove: InterVarsity, 1964).

22. Kenyon, *Our Bible and the Ancient Manuscripts*, 23.

CHAPTER 4

1. Joseph Angus, *The Bible Handbook* (London: Religious Tract Society, 1864), 56.

2. Norman L. Geisler and William E. Nix, *A General Introduction to the Bible* (Chicago: Moody Press, 1986), 430.

3. Ibid., 353–354.

4. Ibid., 431.

5. Eusebius, *Ecclesiastical History III*. 39.

6. Irenaeus, *Against the Heresies/St. Irenaeus of Lyons*, translated and annotated by Dominic J., with further revisions by John J. Dillon (New York: Paulist Press, 1992).

7. Tacitus, *Annals, in Great Books of the Western World*, ed. Robert Maynard Hutchins, vol. 15, The Annals and the Histories by Cornelius Tacitus (Chicago: William Benton, 1952), 44.

8. Suetonius, *Life of Claudius* in *The Twelve Caesars*, trans. Robert Graves and revised by Michael Grant (New York: Viking Penguin, 1979), 25.4.

9. Suetonius, *Life of Nero*, in *The Twelve Caesars*, trans. Robert Graves and revised by Michael Grant (New York: Viking Penguin, 1979), 16.

10. Flavius Josephus, *The Antiquities of the Jews* (New York: Ward, Lock, Bowden, 1900), 20.9.1.

11. Julius Africanus, *Chronography*, in *Ante-Nicene Christian Library: Translations of the Writings of the Fathers*, vol. 1 (Edinburgh: T & T Clark, 1867), 18.

12. Pliny the Younger, *Letters*. Translated by W. Melmoth. Quoted in Norman L. Geisler, *Baker Encyclopedia of Christian Apologetics* (Grand Rapids: Baker Book House, 1998), 10:96.

13. Ibid., L, 10:97.

14. Lucian of Samosata, "Death of Pelegrine," in trans. H.W. Fowler and F.G. Fowler, *The Works of Lucian of Samosata*, 4 vols. (Oxford: Clarendon Press, 1949), 11.

15. Gary R. Habermas, *The Historical Jesus* (Joplin: College Press, 1996), 206–207.

16. Ibid., 207.

17. Norman L. Geisler, *Baker Encyclopedia of Christian Apologetics* (Grand Rapids: Baker, 1998), 384–385.

18. Habermas, *The Historical Jesus*, 224.

19. William F. Albright, *The Archaeology of Palestine*, rev. (Baltimore: Penguin, 1960), 127–128.

20. Nelson Glueck, *Rivers in the Desert: History of Negev* (New York: Farrar, Straus, and Cadahy, 1959), 31.

21. John Elder, *Prophets, Idols, and Diggers* (New York: Bobbs Merrill, 1960), 159–160; Joseph P. Free, Archaeology and Bible History (Wheaton: Scripture Press, 1969), 285.

22. Elder, *Prophets, Idols, and Diggers*, 160.

23. Ibid., 159–160; Free, *Archaeology and Bible History*, 285.

24. Free, *Archaeology and Bible History*, 317.

25. F. F. Bruce, *The New Testament Documents: Are They Reliable?* (Downers Grove: InterVarsity Press, 1964), 95; William F. Albright, *Recent Discoveries in Bible Lands* (New York: Funk and Wagnalls, 1955), 118.

26. Geisler, *Baker Encyclopedia of Christian Apologetics*, 47.

27. F. F. Bruce, "Archaeological Confirmation of the New Testament," as cited in ed. Carl Henry, *Revelation and the Bible* (Grand Rapids: Baker, 1969), 325.

28. Ibid., 326.

29. Colin J. Hemer, *The Book of Acts in the Setting of Hellenistic History* (Winona Lake: Eisenbrauns, 1990), 104–107.

30. A. N. Sherwin-White, *Roman Society and Roman Law in the New Testament* (Oxford: Clarendon Press, 1963), 189.

31. E. M. Blaiklock, *The Acts of the Apostles* (Grand Rapids: William B. Eerdmans, 1959), 89.

32. William F. Albright, *The Biblical Period from Abraham to Ezra* (New York: Harper & Row, 1963), 1–2.

33. Ibid., 1–2.

34. Geisler, *Baker Encyclopedia of Christian Apologetics*, 50–51.

35. John Garstang, *The Foundations of Bible History; Joshua, Judges* (New York: R. R. Smith, Inc., 1931), 146.

36. Avaraham Biram, "House of David," in *Biblical Archaeology Review*, March/April 1994, 26.

MORE ON EVIDENCE FOR CHRISTIANITY

JOSH McDOWELL

The NEW EVIDENCE THAT DEMANDS A VERDICT

Evidence I & II
Fully Updated in One Volume
To Answer Questions Challenging
Christians in the 21st Century

Throughout this book we have referred to and quoted material from *The New Evidence That Demands a Verdict*, the revised and updated version of the classic *Evidence That Demands a Verdict*, which has served as a comprehensive Christian defense resource for more than thirty years. The revised text provides detailed evidential documentation for the reliability of Scripture, the deity of Christ, his resurrection, the case for and against Christianity, and much more.

Specifically in this book we have referred to and drawn from the following chapters of *The New Evidence That Demands a Verdict:*

Part One: The Case for the Bible
3. Is the New Testament Historically Reliable?
4. Is the Old Testament Historically Reliable?

Part Two: The Case for Jesus
5. Jesus, A Man of History
6. If Jesus Wasn't God, He Deserves an Oscar
7. Significance of Deity: The Trilemma–Lord, Liar, or Lunatic?
8. Support of Deity: Old Testament Prophecies Fulfilled in Jesus Christ
9. Support of Deity: The Resurrection–Hoax or History?

Part Four: Truth or Consequences
32. The Nature of Truth
33. The Knowability of Truth
34. Answering Postmodernism

Available wherever Christian books are sold.
Published by Thomas Nelson Publishers, Nashville, Tennessee
www.thomasnelsonpublishers.com

About the Authors

JOSH McDOWELL is an internationally known author and speaker and traveling representative for Campus Crusade for Christ. He has a bachelor's degree in language from Wheaton College and a master's degree in theology from Talbot Theological Seminary.

Josh has spoken to more than ten million young people in eighty-four countries on more than 700 university and college campuses. He has authored or coauthored more than one hundred books and workbooks with more than forty-two million in print worldwide. Josh's most popular works are *The New Evidence That Demands a Verdict, More Than a Carpenter, Right from Wrong, Don't Check Your Brains at the Door, Beyond Belief to Convictions,* and *The Last Christian Generation.*

Josh has been married to his wife Dottie for more than thirty-four years and has four children. Josh and Dottie live in Dana Point, California.

THOMAS WILLIAMS' eleven books include fiction, theology, and drama, among them his three medieval novels, *The Crown of Eden, The Devil's Mouth,* and *The Bride of Stone,* the nonfiction *The Heart of the Chronicles of Narnia,* the best-selling *Knowing Aslan,* and the Gold Medallion award finalist *In Search of Certainty,* co-written with Josh McDowell. Williams, an award-winning artist, has designed or illustrated more than 1500 book covers for many of the major Christian publishers. He served as executive art director for Word Publishing for fourteen years before he began writing full-time and providing consulting and creative services to book publishers.

Tom and his wife, Faye, have three married daughters and eight grandchildren. They live in Granbury, Texas, near Fort Worth.